INDIGENOUS HISTORICAL KNOWLEDGE

Kautilya and His Vocabulary

VOLUME II

INDIGENOUS HISTORICAL KNOWLEDGE

Kautilya and His Vocabulary

VOLUME II

Editors

Pradeep Kumar Gautam

Saurabh Mishra

Arvind Gupta

INSTITUTE FOR DEFENCE STUDIES & ANALYSES
NEW DELHI

PENTAGON PRESS

Indigenous Historical Knowledge: Kautilya and His Vocabulary

Pradeep Kumar Gautam, Saurabh Mishra and Arvind Gupta (Editors)

First Published in 2016

ISBN 978-81-8274-866-8

Published by
PENTAGON PRESS
206, Peacock Lane, Shahpur Jat,
New Delhi-110049
Phones: 011-64706243, 26491568
Telefax: 011-26490600
email: rajan@pentagonpress.in
website: www.pentagonpress.in

Branch
Flat No.213, Athena-2,
Clover Acropolis,
Viman Nagar,
Pune-411014
Email: pentagonpresspune@gmail.com

In association with
Institute for Defence Studies and Analyses
No. 1, Development Enclave,
New Delhi-110010
Phone: +91-11-26717983
Website: www.idsa.in

Printed at Aegean Offset Printers, Greater Noida, U.P.

Contents

About the Contributors

1. Amb. Shivshankar Menon was the National Security Advisor to the Prime Minister of India from 2010-2014 and Foreign Secretary of India from 2006 to 2009. He has served as Ambassador and High Commissioner to Israel, Sri Lanka, China and Pakistan. He was also seconded to the Department of Atomic Energy in the early eighties and was a member of the Atomic Energy Commission 2008-14. His professional experience was concentrated on India's neighbours, atomic energy and disarmament, and India's relations with the major powers. Menon speaks Chinese and some German. He has an M.A. degree in History with specialisation in Ancient India.

2. Dr. Arvind Gupta is the Deputy National Security Adviser at the National Security Council Secretariat, Government of India. Earlier, he was the Director General of Institute for Defence Studies and Analyses (IDSA) from 2012-14 and held the Lal Bahadur Shastri Chair on National Security at the IDSA (2008-12). He retired from the Indian Foreign Service (IFS) after serving in the Ministry of External Affairs and Missions abroad in different capacities. He has attended a number of security conferences in India and abroad and written extensively on diplomatic and security issues.

3. Dr. Jayashree Vivekanandan is Assistant Professor, South Asian University, New Delhi.

4. Dr. Medha Bisht is Assistant Professor, South Asian University, New Delhi.

5. Wing Commander G. Adityakiran was Instructor, Defence Service Staff College, Wellington, Tamil Nadu, India. He is now on active service in the field.

6. Group Captain Vinay Vittal was posted at Air HQ, New Delhi. He is now on active service in the field.

7. Wing Commander U.C. Jha (Retd.) is Ph.D. in Law and Governance from JNU, New Delhi.

8. Col. Harjeet Singh (Retd.) is the author of *The Military Strategy of the Arthaśāstra*.

9. Col. Pradeep Kumar Gautam (Retd.) is Research Fellow at IDSA, New Delhi and convener of the seminar.

10. Dr. Saurabh Mishra is a Research Assistant at IDSA, New Delhi.

Introduction

This volume is the second publication on Kautilya's *Arthasastra*. The first volume consisted of papers presented in various seminars and interactions held on the topic.[1] It was highlighted in these seminars and discussions that there was a need for more application of the research work done on the *Arthasastra*.

As a result, a reference desk was set up in the IDSA library containing root texts as that of R.P. Kangle and others, which were widely read and referred to. A web portal has since been created on the web pages of IDSA titled 'Project—Indigenous Historical Knowledge'.[2]

Shri Shivshankar Menon, who was the National Security Adviser (NSA), delivered the Keynote Address as he had done in the previous seminar in October 2012. A reading of the two keynotes clearly shows that there is a need for us to be more conscious of our traditions and much more work needs to be done to establish scholarship in our traditional strategic culture. An interesting fact which the former NSA highlighted was that since Kautilya's time theories have multiplied and changed, but politics has not.

To give the project a wider coverage, the help of Indian Council of Social Science Research (ICSSR) was sought. With the sponsorship of the ICSSR a set of scholars were invited to present their work in October 2013. To locate and map scholars who have used the text to explain contemporary issues combined with a working knowledge of the text was no easy job. We only nominated scholars who had some published work in this domain related to our aim of covering security related issues. Meanwhile, as a result of the two workshops held at the IDSA in October 2012 and April 2013 and other published articles in the public domain, interest picked up in the reinterpretation of the Kautilya's *Arthasastra*.

To further supplement and raise more pertinent research challenges, the then NSA Shri Shivshankar Menon, in his inaugural lecture at the Jawaharlal Nehru University (JNU) on 'Strategic Culture and International Relations in India' on December 11, 2013, wondered on a simple question: "If India's practice and style of foreign policy is so recognisably and so uniquely Indian, why is there not an Indian theory to explain it?" He argued that one way of developing such a theory is to look back. He then gave example of Chinese scholarship in its endeavour for a similar reinterpretation of the past. The former NSA then placed the challenge before the audience and said, "In India too some people have started this exercise. The IDSA has been sponsoring some truly valuable work on Kautilya and the *Arthasastra*. It is interesting in showing how central the state was to strategic thinking in India as early as the third century BC, long before other cultures stopped speaking of a mysterious God and his way as central to strategy. This is extremely useful work, if nothing else, to break the mental shackles of academic and linguistic conditioning. But it has its limits." He then suggested looking at the present and moving forward. To deal with new issues, it is essential that we elaborate our own rich culture and tradition of strategic thought and build on it.[3] The need for a rigorous work regime is then clearly laid out. We may say that these are very elementary steps and only the tip of the iceberg has been seen.

It has been well-established that there are three layers of audience or 'customers' for such work. The three user levels are: academics, practitioners and the popular. In our endeavour to conduct a series of events, we have similarly gathered presentations and articles. At the popular level, the videos were uplinked soon after the seminar and are now widely seen and heard. To these films we now present selected papers for the academics and practioners.

This volume begins with the opening remarks by the Director General followed by the Keynote Address by Shri Shivshankar Menon. The volume brings forward selected papers as chapters. We have selected papers on two themes. The first is International Relations and strategic culture, and the second deals with matters related to strategy, art and laws of war.

It is hoped that this short second volume, when read with the first, will expose the reader to the depth and scope of concepts and ideas in the text. Nothing is static and it is further expected that readers may see, for themselves, various chapters on how scholars have interpreted the text with commentaries or *bhashya*. By this, the traditional historical knowledge remains updated, improved and relevant.

In this volume also, for transliteration of the Sanskrit words into English, we have not used the diacritical marks, as in the word *Arthaśāstra* for example. The papers in the book have used it as the *Arthashastra* or *Arthasastra*, as spelt by the authors. However, in some places, the authors have used diacritical marks while referring to texts. We have kept them as they are.

Editors

NOTES

1. Pradeep Kumar Gautam, Saurabh Mishra and Arvind Gupta (eds.), *Indigenous Historical Knowledge: Kautilya and His Vocabulary, Volume-I*, Pentagon Press, New Delhi, 2015.
2. http://idsa.in/history/index.html
3. National Security Adviser Shivshankar Menon on Strategic Culture and IR Studies in India at JNU Convention Centre, New Delhi, December 11, 2013, *Strategic Digest*, 44(1), January 2014, pp. 22-27.

Opening Remarks by Dr. Arvind Gupta, DG, IDSA, at the National Seminar on "Developing Indigenous Concepts and Vocabulary: Kautilya's *Arthasastra*"

October 8, 2013

National Security Adviser Shri Shivshankar Menon,

Friends,

In October last year, we had launched the research project on *The Arthasastra*. We had the honour of welcoming Shri Menon to inaugurate that seminar. We are honoured to have him with us once again on the occasion of this workshop on "Developing Indigenous Concepts and Vocabulary: Kautilya's *Arthasastra*."

In his inaugural address last year, Shri Shivshankar Menon had exhorted the strategic community to develop an Indian discourse on international relations and security studies. This is not an easy task. But, this has to be done. I am happy to say that a systematic study of Kautilya's *Arthasastra*, carried over the last one year, has amply revealed that the *Arthasastra* is rich in ideas, concepts and methodologies useful in the art of governance. Many key messages of the *Arthasastra* are of universal nature, as is the case with the teachings of numerous ancient Indian texts.

We need to cull out those ideas and contextualise them to modern conditions. In fact, modern rulers will do well to benchmark their abilities, capabilities, strategies, performance and analyses against the high standards Kautilya sets for them.

So dominant has been the influence of the *Arthasastra* that many subsequent thinkers and writers through the centuries used the *Arthasastra* as a reference point for their own commentaries and analyses. *Nitisara* of Kamandaki of the 8th century can be cited as an example.

The *Arthasastra* is a rich treasure of principles of statecraft. We need to redeem this treasure for modern usage. Divided into fifteen books, each book containing numerous chapters and *sutras*, the text deals with varied facets of statecraft in great detail. Together, the books cover subjects like training of kings, duties of judges and other functionaries of the state. It deals with the important issues of war, foreign policy, the art of spying, circle of kings, calamities, the science of *tantra* and how to deal with weaker, stronger or treacherous kings or how to manage tranquility on the borders and keep internal peace. The *vijigisu*, the king who aspires to expand his influence surviving among enemies and their allies and becomes a *chakravartin* king, is given a complete course in strategy and tactics that can teach a trick or two to the modern strategicians (strategists) heavily influenced by Barry Buzans, Kenneth Waltzs, and Henry Kissingers of the world. The emphasis all along is on knowledge, knowledge and more knowledge.

Even in the modern context of foreign policy, diplomacy and security, the six attributes of foreign policy (*sadgunya*), or the *mandala* theory of alliances, or the four *upayas* or the commandments of sovereignty are universal. The *mandala* theory is essentially a theory of balance of power among states. Similarly, the classical text has a lot useful to say to even today's spymaster and soldier.

Clearly, it is no one's case that the *Arthasastra* should be applied in toto, unthinkingly, to modern situations. Nor is the argument that the Western thinking should be replaced by ancient *Chanakya Niti*, sustainable. But, a deeper study of the *Arthasastra*, which should be made compulsory reading for our diplomats, soldiers, administrators, will provide an Indian perspective to the art of governance and policy-making.

So far, the *Arthasastra* has been studied by a narrow group of Sanskrit scholars, historians and political scientists but only marginally, and mostly academically. That is hardly enough. It is only now that Chanakya is beginning to be used as a text even in management studies. The Chanakya institute in Mumbai is training budding politicians, and policy-makers in *Chanakyaniti*.

This is a welcome development. But a note of caution is in order. The study of the *Arthasastra* should be based on authentic texts and translations and dispassionate and critical commentaries. Further, the *Arthasastra* is only one of many texts. There are many regional texts on strategy which are of great value too. These must also be studied. The distorted versions of the *Arthasastra*, currently in circulation, can do more harm than good.

It is heartening to note that as result of last year's seminar and subsequent efforts of the IDSA, we have been able to network with a group of international and Indian scholars who have interest in the *Arthasastra*. We will hopefully be able to rebut the Western argument that Indians lack a culture of strategic thinking. The *Arthasastra* and many subsequent texts reveal that Indians could think strategically. But it is equally true that these texts have been neglected in the Indian courses and curricula on security and strategic studies as well as in the training institutions of the country where heavy reliance is placed on foreign ideas and thought. This situation must change.

The *Arthasastra* should be reclaimed as a global and not merely a nationalistic text. It should find its place alongside Sun Tzu, Clausewitz and others. This can happen only if Indian scholars study the text seriously and dispassionately.

We have been able to contact a number of international scholars who have had long standing interest in Chanakya and the *Arthasastra*. These include Thomas Trautmann, Sheldon Pollock, Mark McClish, Michael Liebig, Rashed Uz Zaman, Jean Claude Galey and Partick Olivelle. The last named author and scholar has refined Kangle's seminal translation and study of the *Arthasastra*.

Following last year's seminar, the IDSA organised a workshop in April this year where we involved a number of Indian scholars who study the *Arthasastra*. It was heartening to see some young officers of the Indian armed forces have acquired deep knowledge of the *Arthasastra* and have started applying this to contemporary reality. We are also in the process of publishing the proceedings of last year's seminar.*

We are grateful to the ICSSR for their support in holding the present seminar. I would request, through the NSA, the key ministries and agencies of the Government of India to support and take forward the study of the *Arthasastra*.

I thank the NSA for his presence today. We do hope that his personal encouragement and the support of the Government of India for the project will continue and increase.

Thank you.

*Since published as Vol. I.

Keynote Address by Shri Shivshankar Menon, National Security Adviser

October 8, 2013

Dr. Arvind Gupta, Director IDSA,

Ladies and Gentlemen.

Thank you for asking me to speak at this seminar on Developing Indigenous Concepts and Vocabulary: Kautilya's *Arthashastra*. This is indeed a welcome initiative that the IDSA is carrying forward. I was impressed by the range of scholarship reflected in the papers that are being presented here and look forward to reading them. We have come a long way in the year since your first seminar. My congratulations to Arvind Gupta and all those who have contributed to this exercise.

Your seminar is a welcome initiative because, in my opinion, the study of Kautilya is one of the significant ways in which we can become more self-conscious about the strategic culture that we have, and in which we can contribute to its evolution. Too much of our earlier scholarship on the *Arthashastra* attempted to apply the *Arthashastra* mechanically or formulaically to present policy dilemmas or issues, such as how to deal with Pakistan or our nuclear policy. This may yield some useful insights in a tactical sense. In fact, it is my belief that the results of a Kautilyan analysis would not be very different from our present nuclear policy or policy towards Pakistan. But the larger point is that a mechanical application of "Kautilyan" formulae to our present condition does not contribute to building our capability to think strategically. Your seminar, on the other hand, will do so.

What then should we be studying of the *Arthashastra*?

Exactly what you are proposing to do – the concepts and, even more significantly, the ways of thinking that the *Arthashastra* reveals. This is useful because in many ways the world which we face today, (of multiple states, of several major powers, of an uneven but lumpy distribution of power among those major states even while the system has one predominant military power), is similar to the world that Kautilya operated in when he built the Mauryan Empire to greatness. There are no exact parallels in history, but there are certainly ways of thinking conditioned by context and similar circumstance. While our technologies and experiences may be very different from those Kautilya knew, human nature, politics and state behaviour do not appear to have changed quite as much or so drastically as to be unrecognisable. In other words, since Kautilya's time, theories have multiplied and changed drastically, politics has not.

That may explain why the *Arthashastra* is so integral to our strategic culture, and to the ways in which the ordinary Indian thinks of these issues. The *Arthashastra* is certainly not the only work that has shaped our strategic culture, for there are other works from the past, like the *Shantiparva* of the *Mahabharata*, that also play a formative role in popular thinking. Besides, the modern Western overlay of the nineteenth and twentieth century on our academic thinking is now very strong. But there is no gainsaying the fundamental importance of the *Arthashastra* in our thinking. Kautilyan ideas of *mandalas*, of the basic functions of the state, of the necessity and justification for the use of force, and of *raisons d'etat*, are part of the popular vocabulary and thinking on politics and international relations in India. Much of this is unselfconscious and instinctive today. Your work here is, therefore, important in bringing us to the next stage of self-aware thinking on these issues.

The last few years have already seen considerable progress in this direction. Since the time when the IDSA's Director K. Subrahmaniam ploughed a lonely furrow, there has been a significant increase in the number of Indian scholars, think-tanks and institutions teaching, researching and commenting on strategic issues. The problem now is not one of quantity but of quality, of coherence, and of analytical rigour in that effort. Most important is the issue of relevance to Indian conditions and needs, which cannot result from the wholesale borrowing of concepts and ways of thinking from abroad. I welcome the IDSA continuing to lead this effort, as it has from the beginning, and am most impressed by all that you have done under Arvind Gupta's leadership to achieve these goals.

With these few words, let me wish you success and fulfillment in your work on Kautilya, encourage the IDSA to continue this good work, and wish your seminar great success.

Thank you.

PART I

DISCOURSE ON INTERNATIONAL RELATIONS AND STRATEGIC CULTURE

1

The Text as Tradition: Interpreting India's Strategic History

Jayashree Vivekanandan

Why does the text command an exalted status in historical narratives? How are textual representations of historical memory theorised, especially in charting their contemporary relevance? The paper takes as its point of departure the privileging of the notion of tradition in International Relations (IR) theory, of which the text forms an integral part. By arraying thinkers to constitute a formidable phalanx, the tradition forges an unbroken intellectual lineage that connects the past to the present. Texts codifying the collective wisdom of the ages are regarded as critical to this intellectual exercise. The paper reads Kautilya's *Arthashastra* from this theoretical vantage point.[1] It asserts that the centrality of the treatise to interpreting India's strategic history needs to be examined in the light of two interrelated processes. Colonial enquiries into India's past lent credence to the claim that the ancient period epitomised the quintessential essence of Indian culture. This orientation finds powerful resonance in the contemporary literature on India's strategic culture, engaged as it is in a search for continuities with the past. The strategic significance of the *Arthashastra*, the paper argues, is integrally connected to the return of history in such cultural explanations of state behaviour. It suggests an alternative reading of the *Arthashastra* that is attentive to historical context and avoids the teleological orientation typical of trans-historical interpretations.

Sanctifying Tradition

Theorists and historians alike often betray a shared penchant to trace a given idea in its developed form back in time. Quentin Skinner refers to this tendency as 'the mythology of doctrines', wherein an idea assumes an identity independent of its evolutionary history.[2] A selective reading of history is then reduced to "searching for approximations to the ideal type" and "pointing out earlier 'anticipations' of later doctrines."[3] To pluck an idea out of its context is to effectively lose track of its deviations in history. IR theory has likewise tended to approach concepts such as sovereignty and the international system in their evolved manifestations. Julie Reeves asserts:

> "Understanding the heritage behind concepts…sheds light on our knowledge of the history of the IR discipline….The idea that idealism begat realism begat neo-realism and a whole load of critiques is too simplistic; at worst it creates the impression that the subsequent set of ideas are an improvement on the latter, which may not always be the case."[4]

For a field that has long been charged with nurturing a historically impoverished view of the world, IR theory has done little to address the lacuna. Notwithstanding the ritual nod to interdisciplinarity, mainstream theories have preferred to mine history for illustrative instances to validate claims. Further, the quest for historical cases has been driven more by the need to seek similarities between previous political orders and the present state system than explain the differences.

The key concept that has ensured a continuist approach within IR is that of the 'tradition' which stretches back to the ancient period. The notion of tradition, entailing the 'retrospective analytical construction which produces a rationalised version of the past' is most prevalent in political theory, spin-offs from which are evident in IR theory as well.[5] In a retrospective positioning of philosophers, IR laid claim to an exalted lineage in international politics. Thus, a formidable phalanx of thinkers ranging from Thucydides and Machiavelli to Hobbes provided for an unbroken intellectual tradition to which later writers such as Carr and Morgenthau contributed. The compulsions behind constructing a grand tradition are rooted in contemporary concerns.[6] Texts occupy a central position in this intellectual exercise of 'writing history backwards', interested as its proponents are in substantiating their own theoretical claims by pointing out their historical antecedents.[7] Nonetheless, there is growing recognition within IR to be more mindful of complexity and contingency in its case studies.[8] Robert Gilpin's belief that "the past is not merely a prologue and that the present does not have a monopoly on the truth" is indicative of this trend.[9] Increased historical content in IR literature has however not meant that IR has rid itself of the charge of being 'ahistorical'. This is largely on account of the continuing and often compulsive need to find similarity with the contemporary international system. The search for fixed interpretations has meant that IR theory chose to foreswear openness as a path to historicity.[10] Nowhere is this 'problem of history' more evident than in the treatment of postcolonial societies such as India within IR.

The paper seeks to locate the strategic significance of Kautilya's *Arthashastra* in the context of two inter-related strands of scholarship: the colonial enquiries into Indian history and the contemporary literature on India's strategic culture. Admittedly, both trends pertain to very different time scales and also cover somewhat disparate subject areas. The extensive and systematic studies undertaken made colonialism a truly interdisciplinary pursuit, spanning diverse fields encompassing geography, psychiatry, anthropology and history. The scholarship on Indian strategic culture is both more recent and specific in comparison. However, they both share a similar orientation towards Indian history; one that gives primacy to the ancient period over other eras. The assumption that the ancient period held the key to understanding contemporary concerns is implicit in both strands. So is the premise that there exist enduring continuities between the ancient and the modern periods that make trans-historical comparisons a worthwhile pursuit. The following section locates current attempts at examining the relevance of the *Arthashastra* within this broader intellectual context.

Colonial Interventions

Theorising interstate relations has had a long history in India. Indigenous writings on statecraft and diplomacy date back to ancient India when strategists such as Kautilya theorised in a political milieu of multiple independencies. The medieval period saw another exposition of India's strategic practice with the incorporation of the Islamic theory of state; one that placed the state squarely within the ambit of a heterogeneous society. It is ironical that despite this long and sustained history of strategic thought, it was the European theorisations that went on to dominate subsequent studies on India. The anomaly can be readily explained by the existence of an elaborate colonial apparatus that provided the support structure, and indeed, the *raison d'etre* for European investigations. Indology and its attendant variants were intrinsically linked to the colonial project and hence emerged as an organised body of knowledge covering areas ranging from religion to language.

The manner in which Indian history came to be periodised and textualised during the colonial period was to have significant implications on the shaping of India's national identity. Orientalists such as William Jones believed in the potential of the texts to lead the way back to the essence of Hindu civilisation from the present state of depravity that the natives were believed to be living in. The search for India's 'pure' essence in the ancient period arose, as Nietzsche puts it "from the belief that things are most precious and essential at the moment of birth."[11] This assumption stems from the anthropological approach to culture, in which the 'native' acquires central importance in its conceptualisation. The 'native' in colonial literature was the quintessential Hindu who represented the resilience of ancient Indian civilisation to repeated invasions.[12] Ancient India was taken to be the essence of Indian culture and was privileged over its living representation. As Thapar notes:

> "Histories of the 'Hindu' religion have been largely limited to placing texts and ideas in a chronological perspective with few attempts at relating these to the social history of the time. Scholarship also tended to ignore the significance of the popular manifestation of religion in contrast to the textual..."[13]

Indeed, the colonial penchant for making a virtue out of the aloofness that the written word afforded is reflected in James Mill's assertion:

> "What is worth seeing or hearing in India, can be expressed in writing. As soon as everything of importance is expressed in writing, a man who is duly qualified may obtain more knowledge of India in one year, in his closet in England, than he could obtain during the course of the longest life, by the use of his eyes and his ears in India."[14]

The hunt for the pure essence of Indian culture led the colonialists to look beyond the native, at certain classical texts of ancient India. Orientalism systematised Hinduism through textualisation, i.e. the exercise of seeking the essence of a religion in certain sacred texts. Extant Brahmanical discourses stressing on the timeless quality of Indian culture provided the philosophical foundation upon which the elaborate Orientalist discourse on Indian culture came to be subsequently constructed. The two key texts that according to the British held the key to India's identity were Manu's *Dharmashastras* and the *Bhagavad Gita*. Translated in the eighteenth century by Jones and Charles Wilkins respectively, the treatises were taken to be representative of Hinduism. Wilkins' translation of the *Bhagavad Gita* in 1785 paved the way for the privileging of the text in a manner that was to have a profound influence on Orientalist and nationalist perceptions of Indian philosophy. The notion of the *Gita* as a scripture representative of and befitting an ancient civilisation was upheld by the nationalists, and thereafter gained widespread political legitimacy. The role the Orientalists played was indeed central to the entire process of the systematic textualisation that followed.[15]

Extant epics and Vedic texts are significant to our discussion of Kautilya here especially given their rich repertoire of incisive references to military and political affairs, strategising and war-making. A notable attribute of India's philosophical literature (taken to be the mainstay of its culture by strategic culturalists) is the marked paucity of treatises devoted to military affairs. If a researcher were to embark upon a search for historical military texts, she would come upon few other than the *Arthashastra*.[16] That the bulk of such material is couched in ostensibly religious and sacred literature perhaps indicates a self-conscious desire to define security in holistic terms.

Contemporary Interpretations

India presents us with an interesting interface between theory and history; its rich strategic history remaining surprisingly understudied in IR theory. The British Committee, with its avowed objective 'to make past history continuous with present experience, and to see how far the more long-term views or surveys of the historian might affect one's appreciation of the present day', was concerned with studying the historical origins of international politics.[17] Adam Watson, a member of the British Committee, hailed the *Arthashastra* for being a 'major theoretical analysis of international relations as an integral part of the problems of statecraft', a fusion unparalleled in contemporary history.[18] Kautilya's distinction between the mediatory king (*madhyama*) and the neutral king (*udasina*) is a sign of political sophistication, which

> "...may be the first instance in a text of the concept of neutrality, and of the steps which a conqueror or someone resisting conquest should adopt towards a neutral state. No such distinctions between a mediatory and a neutral power are to be found in the writings of the near east or Greece; and the European system rarely got beyond allies, enemies and neutrals."[19]

Since kingship in the *Arthashastra* was not concerned with divinity, the power to wage war was released from the logic of *dharma* and the attendant duties expected of the virtuous king. Watson points out that for Kautilya:

> "...the end of power was not the service of the gods or an ideology, but the happiness of the state. He believed...that a multitude of independencies was not the most desirable state of affairs, and that on the contrary greater happiness could be attained by establishing a benevolent imperial rule. It is curious that from the *Arthashastra* to the American Declaration of Independence (which opposes imperial rule) no other text puts the pursuit of happiness quite so high."[20]

Within the field of IR, particularly in writings that attempted to give a cultural slant to India's influence, the constructed colonial images have been by and large accepted uncritically. Milton Singer, who was closely involved with the Chicago project, argued that India's 'sacred centre' was its ancient 'Sanskritic tradition'.[21] The Chicago project was basically driven by the same concerns that occupied the minds of the Orientalists—to uncover an underlying tradition that would draw divergent cultural strands into one composite Indian culture. However, George Tanham's essay on Indian strategic thought is arguably the most comprehensive contemporary reflection of Orientalist images of India and their strategic significance.[22] While their faith in *dharma*, *karma* and transmigration leads Indians to nurture 'a passive, almost fatalistic acceptance of life', the caste system as the 'bedrock' of Indian society further 'tends to foster a conservative and non-innovative mind-set...'[23] Studies seeking to refute claims of a defensive India also reflect the tendency to delineate identifiable attributes that have survived the ravages of history. A culturally militaristic Indian outlook is located in certain key ancient texts such as the *Arthashastra*, *Manusmriti* and the *Vedas*.[24] Andrew Latham asserts that the Kautilyan tradition prevents Indian decision-makers from exploring shared interests with Pakistan that could become the basis for initiating Confidence Building Measures.[25]

Clearly, contemporary literature continues to be largely informed by societalism that tends to reduce political, economic and religious phenomena to social processes, and upon which much of Orientalist writings were based.[26] The scholarship on India's strategic history, whether in stressing on a defensive orientation or a realist predisposition, is marked by the proclivity to regard history and culture as a seamless whole from which validations of contemporary positions can be sought.

Historicising Diplomacy

An essential aspect towards understanding the nature of India's strategic practice is the approach ancient India adopted towards warfare and diplomacy. A disclaimer at this juncture is necessary that the attempt here is not to trace the 'native' or 'indigenous' theorisations on statecraft before the 'disruptions' caused by invasions during the medieval period followed. As with any other country, these invasions brought with them diverse ways of thinking about war and peace, thereby contributing to the evolution of strategic thinking in the subcontinent. However, this is not to discount the importance of theorisations that existed in ancient India. As Adam Watson asserts, "No system of diverse states and peoples developed a greater sophistication in ancient times than that of India."[27] Although many of the ideas prevalent then may be lost in contemporary times, they would serve as a useful beginning towards theorising about strategic practice in India.

Ethics of war in ancient India came to be shaped by a parallel engagement with the traditions of heroism and prudence. The near simultaneous interest in contrasting types is evident in the growth of both the *dharmashastra* and the *arthashastra* literatures. Whereas the former stressed on the ethical behaviour expected of a king, the latter served as injunctions to the ruler regarding the conduct of statecraft. The dichotomy between the two traditions is reflected in the contrasting genres of literature that contained these ideas. The tradition stressing on *dharma* was chiefly located in epic literature, as against the genre of writing emphasising prudence which found expression in the literature on statecraft.[28] Unlike the Christian tradition which was specifically engaged with the just war theory, the *dharmashastra* tradition believed that the ethics on warfare were informed by the duties of the ruler, and as such were part of the larger scheme of *rajadharma*. The enlightened ruler, who was aware of the ethical dimensions of violence, was endowed with divine attributes that enabled him to wield his power to wage war with discretion. The king in India was seen as an extension of God and as such was bestowed with the attributes of the divine cosmos.[29] His authority was distinct from that of his European counterpart whose right to rule was a conferment by God. The rationale behind vesting warfare with the significance of kingship duties rests on the concept of *karmayoga*. *Karmayoga* elevates the status of warfare to the level of a sacrifice expected of a virtuous ruler. The *Mahabharata* saw the war as a sacrificial act (*yuddhayagna*), aspects of which were comparable to those of a conventional sacrifice.[30] The constraints on the power of the king were in some senses unique to the Indian notion of kingship itself.

Notwithstanding the duality of power in terms of the temporal and the religious domains in the Christian and Muslim world, both realms were located within the same social sphere. In contrast, the Indian worldview restricted the authority of the king by postulating the sphere of renunciation over which he had little control but which legitimised his divine status in the temporal realm. The *brahmin*, by renouncing the social sphere stood independent of it, because of which his sphere lay beyond the grasp of the king.[31] The contradiction between the circumscribed powers of the king and the stricture that he was to have the final word on matters of *dharma* can be explained in terms of the amorphous nature of *dharma* itself. Howsoever great its appeal, the application and observance of *dharma* required the institutionalised support of an organisational apparatus, which the king alone could provide.[32]

As opposed to the *dharmashastra* literature which supported divine kingship, the *arthashastra* genre upheld the theory of contractual kingship, stressing on resorting to war in order to attain state objectives such as security. According to Kautilya, "*Artha* is the source of the livelihood of human beings, in other words, the earth inhabited by men. The science which is the means of the attainment and protection of that earth is the *Arthashastra.*"[33] A template of twelve kings makes up Kautilya's *mandala* theory arrayed along alternating zones of alliance and hostility. The existence of twelve kings is not a necessary precondition for the *mandala* logic to work; instead, they personify the entire range of relationships that are likely to emerge with the conqueror's attempts at expansion.[34]

Consequently, war was not a sacrificial act validated by honourable intentions and just means, but was one of the many courses available to the king to achieve other ends. Other than expansion by conquest, Kautilya also envisaged settlement on unoccupied territory (*sunyanivesa*) as a mode of spreading the imperial frontiers. Although unoccupied territory was in principle the domain of the king, facilitating the formation of villages on virgin lands was postulated as a significant state activity.[35] Kautilya's emphasis on expediency often entailed winning the support and confidence of conquered people. He counselled the granting of considerable degrees of local autonomy and to leave local power structures in conquered areas undisturbed to facilitate a peaceful transition. Peace and even neutrality in war was to be preferred as it entailed the most judicious use of state resources. That said, even in peacetime, every state should be prepared for war and for which no means were to be spared.

Kautilya also refrained from making a stark demarcation between the internal and external realms of a state. Instead, what was central to his calculation was the proximity of the enemy, evident from his assertion that 'the *janapada* [kingdom] is shared with the enemy.' Given that the domain of the king is not clearly demarcated, the strategies Kautilya suggested were thus the same for dealing with both internal sedition and external invasion. Since the enemy existed both within and beyond a king's domain, strategists like Kautilya and Manu did not advise the use of force as the primary state instrument. Indeed, coercion was less favoured than sedition in terms of potency and effectiveness in countering enemies. The reason behind force being attributed less significance lay in the nebulous nature of sovereignty. As Andre Wink notes:

> "The conquest which is desired by the conqueror-to-be is not primarily a matter of military action, but of expansion of his sovereignty or *svavisaya* by effecting alliances with 'those who are likely to be won over' under the enemy's sovereignty or *paravisaya*."[36]

Political fragmentation was the norm during the ancient and medieval periods, but this however did not imply political chaos as is commonly assumed. Indeed, although ancient India was fragmented into multiple kingdoms, the political landscape formed a chequered board on which Kautilya based his well-developed network of alternating relations of alliance and enmity. Sovereignty in India was a nebulous concept that did not entail the clear demarcation of the king's political realm. Since theoretically, the authority of the king was universal (given that he was seen as the microcosm of the entire cosmos), making a distinction between the internal and the external domains was self-limiting. The logic of the all-encompassing authority of the king extended to the use of force as well. A dualistic understanding of the use of force (of seeing internal violence as sedition and external force as war) was likewise absent in Indian theorisations. Thus, the strategies employed in war against external enemies were similar to those against internal opponents.[37]

The necessity of tackling numerous, dispersed and well-entrenched adversaries had a profound influence on the evolution of strategic traditions in India. Both the realist and moralist traditions wrestled with multiple-actor scenarios that fashioned multi-faceted response strategies. Although both differed in terms of the goals that the state was expected to pursue and the means it was to adopt in their pursuit, the two traditions advocated a calibrated use of force. Force was to be a measure of last resort exercised only after all other options had been exhausted. Thus, it is not surprising that references to the use of brute force at the outset of an adversarial situation are rare in ancient Indian texts belonging to both schools. The Kautilyan emphasis on alliance-building through the *mandala* theory rather than a total reliance on indigenous military capability also reflected the preference for collaborative strategies.[38] Ancient India as a conglomeration of many warring kingdoms presented an ambitious ruler with a political scenario that could potentially dissipate his resources and energies through constant war-making. The most efficient response strategy emphasised accommodation and alliance-building.

In the continuum of kingship, that at one end attributes independent divine qualities to the king such as in ancient Egypt, and on the other regards him as a worldly instrument of the divine force as in ancient China and medieval Europe, the position of the Hindu king falls somewhere in the middle. While he was to submit to the writ of *dharma*, he presided over his kingdom as its supreme power. His kingdom was seen as a microcosm of the grand cosmic order. It was believed that the Cosmic Man who generates the universe, and into whom all its elements must return to be regenerated in cyclic alternation, also creates the king with portions taken from the eight deities of the cosmos. Constituted with the radiance and power of the cosmos, the divinity of the Hindu king is inherent in his person and not bestowed by divine right as in medieval European philosophy. The centrality of the Cosmic Man within the cosmos is replicated in the king who is the font of power, order and creation within his kingdom. The claims of Hindu kings over a universal dominion drew from this conception of the kingdom as containing within it all the elements of the entire earth.[39]

However, the status and authority of the king within his kingdom differ in the Hindu and Islamic traditions. While the Hindu tradition vested the king with the divinity drawn from the gods, this replication of the cosmic power in the king is absent in Islamic thought. The latter chooses instead to remind the king of his instrumental status in the scheme of things. Peter Hardy observes of the Islamic tradition, "It is not by reason of his being, but by reason of his behaviour, that the sultan becomes the means whereby subjects enjoy welfare. The real agent is god."[40] Thus, by inference the authority of the king under Islam is vested in him by God whose divine attributes cannot be replicated in any of his creations, and hence no mortal can aspire to reflect His powers in this temporal world.

Power, therefore, was not traditionally conceived in purely political terms but was inextricably linked to ritual authority. The king was not only the head of the temporal realm, but was also seen as the microcosmic embodiment of all elements of the universe. His position was at once circumscribed and sacred, and thus the location of the Indian state within society was far more complex than that of its European counterpart. This complexity yielded a commensurate emphasis on the material and the ideational dimensions of power by both genres. Thus, we find Kautilya cautioning his king against neglecting the power of symbolism that was recognised and acknowledged by his subjects. Such a layered understanding of power also meant that force was seen as one of the many means available to a ruler. This served to nudge rulers into exploring moderation in conflicts as a common strategy. Issues of security remained recessed within broader issues of stability and good life, and often implied that these were couched in acceptable terms. For instance, the notion of balance, whether personified in the king or implemented as a calibrated response to a conflict situation, frequently came to the fore in Indian politics.[41] Although the modern Indian state conceives of its security in primarily militaristic terms, its emphasis on rhetoric and lofty ideals echoes the compelling need to seek a social and ethical justification of security.

Conclusion

Our discussion brings to the fore the compelling need to locate supposedly 'neutral' notions within historical contexts. Concepts such as power and hegemony hold little meaning outside their socio-historical context, and to attribute contemporary connotations to these would be fallacious. The cultural tropes and practices resorted to for the legitimisation of power, are resonant of a certain way of life unique to that societal context alone. The nature and profile of that society itself may change over time, and so would the terms in which power is conceived of and exercised. History, in that sense, permits us to conceptualise culture in dynamic terms. The history of ideas enables the researcher to go back in time sans the baggage of loaded contemporary meanings and concepts.[42] The connotations that the thinkers of antiquity implied may have long since disappeared, but a historical enquiry reaffirms the fact that the evolutionary path of a particular notion was neither linear nor inevitable. It offers an important corrective to IR theory which often associates concepts with a timeless and eternal quality. The tendency to mine history for substantiations of our contemporary concerns also stems from such contrived linkages with the past.[43] This is particularly true in the case of Indian strategic culture, an area that has thrown up a clutch of caricatures invoking India's pristine antiquity. Historical contingency acts as a check against essentialist interpretations of state behaviour of the kind that are typical of many writings in culture studies today. As the history of ideas has shown us, not only were concepts imparted different meanings, but they also moulded identities differently. It exhorts us to problematise, a task that can be both powerful and disorienting. We realise that what "we may be disposed to accept as 'timeless' truths may be little more than contingencies of our local history and social structure."[44] It allows us to unbundle a number of cultural tropes typically representative of a postcolonial state and often uncritically accepted within IR. The discipline stands enriched if scholars are open-ended in their enquiry of concepts that are not tethered to contemporary interpretations.

NOTES

1. The chapter is drawn from the author's book, *Interrogating International Relations: India's Strategic Practice and the Return of History*, Routledge, New Delhi, 2011.
2. Susanne Rudolph similarly cautions against transposing a contemporary concept into a time frame when it did not exist or carry the same connotations. For instance, what could possibly be interpreted as an 'agent' in the *Arthashastra* is instead termed a 'spy', which presupposes the existence of a highly bureaucratised state machinery—a typically modern construct. The choice of terminology is not an innocent one since such interpretations of history assume the existence of oriental despotisms that were able to exercise their absolutist control through an extensive spy network. See: Susanne Hoeber Rudolph, "Presidential Address: State Formation in Asia-Prolegomenon to a Comparative Study", *The Journal of Asian Studies*, 46 (4), 1987, p. 738.
3. Quentin Skinner, *Visions of Politics, Vol. 1: Regarding Method,* Cambridge University Press, Cambridge, 2002, pp. 60-63. Norbert Elias' sociological approach to the study

of court society in seventeenth and eighteenth century France can be considered a notable work on the history of ideas. For instance, although Elias concedes that "court society is a social formation whose market-value is low", he firmly believes in the "subordination of present-day values" to the valuations prevalent during the historical period under focus. See: Norbert Elias, *The Court Society*, translated by Edmund Jephcott, Basil Blackwell, Oxford, 1983, p. 28.

4. Julie Reeves, *Culture and International Relations: Narratives, Natives and Tourists,* Routledge, London, 2004, p. 5.
5. John Gunnell, "The Myth of the Tradition", *The American Political Science Review,* 72(1), 1978, p. 132.
6. According to Krygier, a tradition constitutes three elements, namely belief in its historical legacy, an authoritative presence, and its inheritance by succeeding generations rather than the mere discovery from a forgotten past. See: Renee Jeffery, "Tradition as Invention: The 'Traditions Tradition' and the History of Ideas in International Relations", *Millennium*, 34(1), 2005, p. 62.
7. Stefan Collini, et al., *That Noble Science of Politics: A Study in Nineteenth Century Intellectual History*, Cambridge University Press, Cambridge, 1983, p. 4.
8. Some of the theorists who have sought to bring greater historical depth to their studies include Buzan and Little (2000); Watson (1992); and Hobden and Hobson (2002). See: Barry Buzan and Richard Little (2000), *International Systems in World History: Remaking the Study of International Relations,* Oxford University Press, New York, 2000; Adam Watson, *The Evolution of International Society: A Comparative Historical Analysis,* Routledge, London, 1992; Stephen Hobden and John Hobson, *Historical Sociology of International Relations,* Cambridge University Press, Cambridge, 2002.
9. Robert Gilpin, *War and Change in World Politics*, Cambridge University Press, New York, 1981, p. 11.
10. Nick Vaughan-Williams, "International Relations and the 'Problem of History'", *Millennium*, 34(1), 2005, p. 136.
11. Cf. Michael Drolet, *The Postmodernism Reader: Foundational Texts,* Routledge, London, 2004, p. 74.
12. The writing of Indian history in a manner that upheld the ancient Hindu civilisation as bearer of the original Indian identity had several significant implications. The Islamic empires that ruled India during the medieval period were seen as foreign impositions that suppressed and eclipsed India's authentic culture. The dichotomising of Indian history along communal lines that constructed narratives based on the categories of the native and the foreign can clearly be traced back to the colonial discourse. See: Perry Anderson, *Lineages of the Absolutist State*, Verso, London, 1979, p. 480.
13. Romila Thapar, "Imagined Religious Communities? Ancient History and the Modern Search for a Hindu Identity", in David Lorenzen (ed.), *Religious Movements in South Asia 600-1800*, Oxford University Press, New Delhi, 2004, p. 335.
14. James Mill, *The History of British India, Vol. 1*, reprinted in 1990, Associated Publishing House, New Delhi, 1918, p. 7.

15. Rosane Rocher, "British Orientalism in the Eighteenth Century: The Dialectics of Knowledge and Government", in Carol Breckenridge and Peter van der Veer (eds.), *Orientalism and the Postcolonial Predicament: Perspectives on South Asia*, University of Philadelphia Press, Philadelphia, 1993, p. 229.
16. Vinay Lal, *The History of History: Politics and Scholarship in Modern India,* Oxford University Press, New Delhi, 2003, p. 37.
17. The British Committee for the Theory of International Politics (1954-85)—under Butterfield and its three coordinators Wight, Watson and Bull—was an eclectic group of fifty members drawn from diverse backgrounds, like historians, journalists, theologians and jurists. The realist orientation underlying the approach of the Committee was evident in Butterfield's opposition to the idealism surrounding the League of Nations. See: Brunello Vigezzi, *The British Committee on the Theory of International Politics (1954-1985): The Rediscovery of History*, translated by Ian Harvey, Edizioni Unicopli, Milan, 2005, pp. v-vii, 19.
18. Adam Watson, *The Evolution of International Society: A Comparative Historical Analysis,* Routledge, London, 1992, p. 79.
19. *Ibid.*, p. 81.

    The mediatory king was one whose territory lay close to both the conqueror and his immediate enemy and who was noncommittal but powerful enough to determine the balance of power within the circle of states. The territory of the neutral king lay beyond this primary set of kings, but who was also sufficiently powerful to either resist or assist the conqueror, his enemy and the mediatory king.

20 *Ibid.*, p. 83.

21. The University of Chicago was the first to emerge as the seat of Indian studies in the US. See: John Roosa, "Orientalism, Political Economy and the Canonisation of Indian Civilisation", in Silvia Federici (ed.), *Enduring Western Civilisation: The Construction of the Concept of Western Civilisation and its "Others"*, Praeger, Westport, 1995, pp. 152-153.
22. George Tanham, "Indian Strategic Thought: An Interpretive Essay", in Kanti Bajpai and Amitabh Mattoo (eds.), *Securing India: Strategic Thought and Practice,* Manohar, New Delhi, 1996.
23. Tanham's opinion is echoed by Brahma Chellaney who similarly alludes to 'the placidly pacifist Hindus and Jains' along with 'complacent Buddhists' in order to reiterate his argument on the tolerant and peace loving nature of Asians. See: Brahma Chellaney, *Asian Juggernaut: The Rise of China, India and Japan*, Harper Collins, New Delhi, 2006, p. 68.
24. Bharat Karnad for instance, contests the caricature of Indians as a culturally defensive people who shirk the use of force, and argues that the texts offer the ruler a gradient of options culminating in war. For Karnad, Indian strategic thinking is characterised by pragmatism that can be traced to the ancient period. History, he asserts, has reiterated the innate Indian proclivity to be calculative and to strategise. The contribution of the medieval era, referred to as 'the Muslim interregnum', was restricted to changes at the tactical and strategic level, while the already established

grand strategic framework remained intact. See: Bharat Karnad, *Nuclear Weapons and Indian Security: The Realist Foundations of Strategy*, Macmillan, London, 2002, pp. 23-24.

25. Andrew Latham, "Constructing National Security: Culture and Identity in Indian Arms Control and Disarmament Practice", in Keith Krause (ed.), *Culture and Security: Multilateralism, Arms Control and Security Building*, Frank Cass, London, 1999, p. 150.
26. Harry Gelber, *Nations out of Empires: European Nationalism and the Transformation of Asia*, Palgrave, New York, 2001, p. 11.
27. Adam Watson, note 18, p. 77.
28. Torkel Brekke, "Between Prudence and Heroism: Ethics of War in the Hindu Tradition", in Torkel Brekke (ed.), *The Ethics of War in Asian Civilisations: A Comparative Perspective,* Routledge, Abingdon, 2006, p. 138.
29. Manu articulated the divine authority of the king, 'For when this world was without a king and people ran about in all directions out of fear, The Lord emitted a king in order to guard his entire (realm), taking lasting elements from Indra, the Wind, Yama, the Sun, Fire, Varuna, the Moon, and (Kubera) the Lord of Wealth. Because a king is made from particles of these lords of the gods, therefore he surpasses all living beings in brilliant energy, and, like the Sun, he burns eyes and hearts, and no one on earth is able even to look at him'. (Cited in Torkel Brekke, note 28, p. 116.)
30. Torkel Brekke, note 28, p. 115.
31. Before the *asvamedha yagna* (a Vedic ritual sacrifice) commences, the king and the *brahmin* ritually exchange their qualities. The king temporarily forsakes his royalty to the *brahmin* who in turn bequeaths him with his power of *brahminhood.* The symbolic alternation enables the king to withdraw to a life in the wilderness befitting an ascetic, while the *brahmin* assumes charge of the temporal sphere. See: J.C. Heesterman, "The Conundrum of the King's Authority", in J.F. Richards (ed.) *Kingship and Authority in South Asia*, Oxford University Press, Delhi, 1998, pp. 33-34.
32. J.C. Heesterman, note 31, pp. 18-22.
33. Kautilya, *Arthashastra*, translated by R. Shamasastry, The Wesleyan Mission Press, Mysore, 1923, pp. 1-2.
34. R.P. Kangle, *The Kautiliya Arthasastra Part III: A Study*, University of Bombay, Bombay, 1965, p. 249.
35. *Ibid.*, p. 168.
36. Andre Wink, *Land and Sovereignty in India: Agrarian Society and Politics under Eighteenth Century Maratha Svarajya*, Cambridge University Press, Cambridge, 1986, p. 15.
37. Torkel Brekke, note 28, pp. 120-121.
38. Adam Watson, note 18, p. 79.
39. Ronald Inden, "Ritual, Authority, and Cyclic Time in Hindu Kingship", in J.F. Richards (ed.), *Kingship and Authority in South Asia*, Oxford University Press, Delhi, 1998, pp. 46-50.

40. Peter Hardy, "Growth of Authority Over a Conquered Political Elite: Early Delhi Sultanate as a Possible Case Study", in J.F. Richards (ed.), *Kingship and Authority in South Asia*, Oxford University Press, Delhi, 1998, p. 228.
41. Ronald Inden, *Text and Practice: Essays on South Asian History*, School of Oriental and African Studies, London, 2006, pp. 132-133.
42. Quentin Skinner, note 3, p. 89.
43. John Gunnell, note 5, p. 133.
44. Quentin Skinner, note 3, p. 89.

2

Revisiting the *Arthasastra*: Back to Understanding IR

Medha Bisht

The Western discourse on International Relations (IR) goes back to the Westphalian notion, when the artificial construct of the nation-state became the primary referent point for theorising international relations. Moreover, the concept of state, legitimacy, power, order, and foreign policy in varying degrees is often traced to Western philosophical tradition, which traces the idea of IR (predominantly realist) back to Thucydides's *Peloponnesian War*. Given the importance of comparative political philosophy in recent years, it would be interesting to explore how the *Arthasastra*, a magnum opus, written around 4th century BCE, could provide insightful shades to some of the key concepts of international relations.

It is in this backdrop that this paper attempts to revisit the *Arthasastra*. While an attempt has been made to analyse the state as an analytical referent point, its engagement as an autonomous actor with the domestic and international environment is studied. The three common variables which are employed to gauge the engagement of the state with its external and internal domain are political virtue (morality), power, and order. These three variables have been isolated for study, as they often inform the broad discourse in international relations. Even though the idea of power, order, political virtue and state find a legitimate place in the text, these concepts have not been illuminated through the lens of the *Arthasastra* and (even if they have been), they have not been related to the broader understanding of these concepts in international relations and political theory. However, the paper intends to interpret the concept of power and order through the understanding of political virtue, as political virtue appears to be the central tenet around which the entire discourse of the *Arthasastra* revolves.

The paper is divided into three sections. The first section would focus on the significance for undertaking comparative studies and the need for establishing a conversation between the Western philosophical tradition and the Eastern philosophical tradition. How the cross conversation adds to an understanding on the broader concepts of International Relations will be the key question for this section. The second section would focus on the concept of state and discuss briefly how the variables of political virtue, order and power are interpreted, inter-related, interconnected and complement each other. The third section will offer some key insights on how the study of the *Arthasastra* could facilitate a 'Kautilyan' understanding of international relations.

I. A Need for Dialogue

Geographical boundaries have always played a divisive role in international relations. While borders created nation states, intellectual traditions stemming from nation states tried shaping the universalistic understanding of certain ideas and concepts at large. Much of the understanding on norms, rights, justice, equality, therefore, stem from Western philosophical tradition. While Chinese, East Asian, African, Hindu and Islamic traditions had their own world views, many of these failed to reflect on the disciplinary discourses, particularly international relations.[1] Even when one compares the dominant schools in IR, realism and its distinct strands held sway over others like liberalism and Marxism. Given the leaning of IR, towards certain approaches and schools of thought, it would be interesting to revisit the dominant discourses on various concepts of IR, and explore how they were different or similar to the non-Western understanding. It is from this perspective that the *Arthasastra* can throw some light on certain key concepts prevalent in IR. What was the philosophical underpinning behind these concepts and do these concepts shed a new light on the understanding of the dominant strands of IR, is something comparative political analysis can throw light upon. The basic assertions, therefore, for undertaking a comparative perspective are:

- Can ideas of rights, justice, power and equality be universal? Is the Western understanding similar to that of the Eastern understanding, or do various cultures inform the priority of certain principles or political choices?
- Concepts generally have their roots in societal structures and their communitarian origins. Are societies similar across regions, space and time? How do societal structures shape the basic ideas of rights, justice and equality and can there be a universal (read Western) explanation for these?
- How much is culture responsible in shaping some of the core questions related to politics? How is the 'political' defined in various societies and can the 'international' be subsumed within the ambit of distinct 'cultural-political' understandings?

While answers to these questions are neither easy nor direct and would require a detailed analysis of sorts, not suited for an elaboration on this occasion, one can broadly agree that comparative studies do enhance a distinct understanding on certain established notions. Even if the broad understanding on concepts across cultures is the same, it is important to explore how they interact and converse with the dominant strands of these concepts. The second section of this paper attempts to undertake such a comparison.

II. The Kautilyan State—Political Virtue, Order and Power

If one closely looks at the Kautilyan state, it can be interpreted from various vantage points. While some scholars have termed it as a welfare state, others describe it as a totalitarian state.[2] The rationale for the explanation goes back to the idea of state which was built around certain tenets, which Kautilya had conceptualised way back around the 4th century BCE.

The central tenet which comes out from a textual analysis of the *Arthasastra* is that the state was a nodal point. Not only is this evident through the *mandala* theory, where the most dominant state was the *vijigisu,* but there are also instances, where the states exercised both sovereignty and enjoyed autonomy at the domestic level. They enjoyed sovereignty because states did not generally interfere in the domestic issues of other states and they enjoyed autonomy because states were distinct from the society, in some ways autonomous from the societal institutions and influence. One can also say, the state was not just an extension of class or elite interests, but had a distinct identity of its own. In Kautilya's *Arthasastra*, for instance, the state comes across as an overarching entity. It was well organised, had a structured mechanism for covert operations and a broad framework to guide foreign policy. It represented "limited state power, and the purpose was to protect the ordered heterogeneity of the Indian society." The state primarily held but not overtly dictated the domestic order.

Apart from the key elements which defined the nature of the state, the state is also described as being constituted of seven pillars. One can describe these core pillars as the capacity of the state to enforce and implement its decisions.The seven constituents of the state were the *Swami, Amatya, Janapada, Durga, Kosha, Danda, and Mitra.* While the first six were the internal elements, the seventh was an external element, broadly related to diplomacy. Kautilya writes, "Before a king actually sets out an expedition of conquest, he has to take steps to guard himself (read the state) against the dangers, which might weaken any constituents of his own state." The first duty of the King (read national interest) therefore is to protect the people in times of natural disaster and from enemies, both internal and external.[3] Regarding the ministers, Kautilya writes that the power of counsel is superior to military strength and with good judgement a king can overwhelm even kings who are mighty and energetic. Kautilya considered weakness in intellectual judgement as much as a disadvantage and weakness in moral resources.[4]

Three objectives identified with the state are: wealth, justice and expansion.[5] It is interesting to note that justice forms the central referent point, as Kautilya writes for wealth and expansion, as *artha* (wealth) followed *dharma*. Thus, according to Kautilyan thought, material wellbeing is only a part of the larger idea of a state. Kautilya also believed that a stable and prosperous state could only be secured through just administration and that stability and justice preceded (or in other words were the pre-conditions or prerequisites for) accumulation of wealth, which is then used to augment the territory.[6]

If one looks at the economic aspect, the Kautilyan state again was an active participant. Details on trade routes (land and water) are well elaborated. Census, audit reports, welfare practices in terms of building wells, etc., are mentioned. Through its tax extracting capacity, state exercised centralised power over its citizens. Economy was considered important as Kautilya writes, "From wealth came the power of *danda*."[7]

Thus, the Kautilyan state was a strong state. Whether it be in the terms of trade, security or ordering social relations. Every aspect was governed through *dharma*; and *danda* (the rod) was employed to regulate the *dharma*. Order thus was closely related to *dharma* and coercive power was an important factor in augmenting state's capacity.

If one moves on to the *mandala* theory from the domestic level, one again finds that the capacity of the state formed an important aspect of the geo-political order. This is because, instead of anarchy or systemic factors shaping the international system, it was the individual capacity of the state which shaped the system (in this case, a system constituted of distinct geo-political orders). The *mandala* theory is so much dependent on the strength of the state actors that one can frame it as a distinct geo-political order. *Mandala* theory consists of the circle of states, consisting of allies, enemies and neutrals. The circle consists of:[8]

- The *vijigisu*: The aspirant, bent upon conquering and to conquer.
- The *ari*: The enemy—one that is situated anywhere on the circumference of the aspirant's territory.
- The *madhyama*: The mediatory—one capable of helping both the belligerent, whether united or disunited, or of resisting them individually.
- The *udasina*: The neutral—the one very powerful and capable of helping the aspirant, the enemy and the mediatory, together or individually or resisting any of them individually.

A parallel can be drawn to the concept of 'geo-political orders' (international grouping), which Benno Teschke advances. According to Teschke, the constitution, operation and transformation of geo-political orders is predicated on the changing identities of the constitutive units.[9] While Benno Teschke, influenced by Marxism, primarily defines the state as an extension of class interests, which he terms as 'social property relations', the state in Kautilyan terms unlike Teschke's conceptualisation was autonomous from that of society and not just an extension of dominant interests.

Thus, while the state was a distinct entity on its own terms, in terms of autonomy and enforcement agency, a significant factor which becomes conspicuous and which guided state action was the idea of political virtue, more appropriately framed through the concept of *dharma*. As stated before, political virtue or *dharma* was the functional element of the state. *Dharma* has been described as an essential component of Hindu political thought. It comes from the Sanskrit word *dhr*, meaning to hold. Broadly understood as the concept which holds the society together, *dharma* had a special place in the Hindu political thought, as the society was held together by each individual and group doing his or her specific duty. For the Hindu political thinkers, the universe is an ordered whole governed by fixed laws. It is characterised by *Rta*, the inviolable order of things. While society becomes an ordered whole when held together by *dharma*, what shapes the societal *dharma* is the *karma* of the individual. It is important to note that the idea of *dharma* and *karma* are deeply related. An individual's *karma* not only determines his caste but also his *dharma*. *Karma* also defines the rightful *dharma* of the individual. In this context, the *dharma* of king directs the broad contours of political virtue—the qualities broadly identified with that of a just king. The idea of morality thus is present in the *Arthasastra* in different degrees. In fact, the concept of political morality captures the idea of morality in *Arthasastra*. Political morality advances the idea of balancing the concept of *dharma* with pragmatism. One can also say that political morality is about thinking strategies or crafting policies, which minimise harm to your own citizens and Kautilya is very categorical in stating that the interest of the state or the population or subjects in general should be prioritised. The idea of a certain action being based on advancing the idea of larger good thus becomes important. The idea of advancing larger good or just cause is really the fulcrum of Kautilyan analysis, when he talks about concepts like power and order and the happiness of the people at large.

Some of the examples in Kautilya's *Arthasastra*, which broadly relate to the idea of political virtue, are:

Yogakshema: Kautilya placed great importance on the welfare of the people and his practical advice to the king on facilitating the happiness of the people was rooted in *dharma*. The advice for the wellbeing of the people is rooted in pragmatism, as he writes, "If people become impoverished, they become greedy and rebellious."[10] Kautilya further points out that internal rebellion is more dangerous than the external one. Therefore, the interest of people should always be the priority of the king.

Artha: Wealth is the means and not the ends. This is what the *Arthasastra* tells us. A good example of this is Kautilya's discussion on 'promotion of economic activity'. Kautilya writes that the king should augment his power by promoting the welfare of the people, for power comes from the country side, which is the source of all economic activity.[11]

Natural calamities, disasters and epidemic: Kautilya's response to unforeseen calamities is also a pointer to how issues of human and socio-economic welfare were prioritised by the state. Kautilya writes, "In times of calamities, the land should not only be capable of sustaining population, but also outsiders, when they come into the kingdom, in times of calamities." Kautilya did foresee the linkage between natural disasters and potential conflicts and epidemics and environmental security came under the ambit of state security. Thus, welfare of the people also included taking adequate health safety measures, as it was directly linked to the prosperity, stability and security of the state. Similarly, during famines, grains from royal stores were distributed, exemption of taxes was made, public works like road constructions were started for the unemployed, rich were heavily taxed and help from foreign countries was also sought.[12]

A common theme which runs across all the aforementioned points is that state interest is defined broadly in terms of the welfare of the population and justification of national interest is based on the fact that it is an extension of the interests of the people at large and the strength of the state is directly contingent on the welfare of the population.

Equally fascinating in the Kautilyan concept of state are the concepts of power, order and political virtue. Significantly, the concept of political virtue greatly informs the concept of order and power. While concept of order is broadly associated with the idea of obedience, duties and responsibility towards the other and the society, power in Kautilyan understanding relates both to the soft and hard interpretations.

The Idea of Order and Power in Kautilan *Arthasastra*

Order and power in the *Arthasastra* are complimentary and feed on each other. The commonality between the two concepts is that both are governed by the idea of political virtue—the idea of just restraint. The difference, however, is that coercive power (force) makes the idea of power distinct from that of order, an option which Kautilya substantively deliberated upon.

Order in the *Arthasastra*

The concept of order has been elaborated and conceptualised by Hedley Bull in *The Anarchical Society.* Bull describes order as a relative concept—defining it broadly as a perceptual means to understand the objective world. For Bull, the idea of order is not "any pattern or regularity in the relations of human individuals and groups, but a pattern that leads to a particular result, an arrangement of social life such that it promotes certain goals and values."[13] For Bull, therefore, order is primarily defined by the *purpose* it serves. In other words, "different set of values or ends" endow meaning to the concept of order. While Bull operationalises this broad definition of order to the societal (domestic) and international realm, the common, overlapping concern at the domestic and the international front is the idea of 'obedience' or conformity to certain set of rules of conduct that order entails.

It is from this perspective that Bull in *The Anarchical Society* defines order as a pattern of behaviour, which underwrites the fundamental goals of social life. He writes, "order in this sense is maintained by a sense of common purpose…by rules, which prescribe the patterns of behaviour that sustain them and by institutions, which make these rules effective."[14] Socialisation of states thus is the primary tool for sustaining order at the international level and also is the key element which enables the transition from an international system to an international society. Diplomacy has been perceived as an important conduit for facilitating order and also a tool to facilitate socialisation between states. Bull delineated four functions of diplomatic activity: (1) to facilitate communication, (2) to help negotiate agreements, (3) to enable the gathering of intelligence and information, (4) and to minimise the effects of friction in international relations.[15] Bull further writes that as diplomatic activity between states flourished, the concept of international society started gaining prominence. International society then denoted a group of states, conscious of certain common international values and conceived themselves to be bound by a general set of rules in their relations with each other. This understanding associated with international society and thus of order has been attributed to the English School of International Relations.

Martin Wight, another proponent of the English School, delineates the theoretical underpinnings of international society and thus of order, into revolutionary and non-revolutionary international politics. Wight considers these two contrasting phenomenon as embedded in three traditions of international political thought which he termed as Realism, Revolutionism and Rationalism. According to realism, as Wight defines it, international politics consists of international anarchy, where the Hobbesian views of war against all proceeds unhindered. He writes that as in the international realm conflict between sovereign states is guided purely by national interest, morality is largely irrelevant. Defining revolutionism and identifying it with the Kantian tradition, he writes that for the Kantians, the ultimate reality is the community of mankind, not the states. Rationalism, defined as the middle way and identified with the Grotian tradition, was considered to be the most relevant to English School. The Grotian tradition believed that though international politics is anarchical, it is mitigated by an international intercourse, a relationship between states characterised not only by conflict but also through cooperation.

It is interesting to note that all the historical antecedents of these schools have been traced to the western philosophical tradition. Little referencing has been made to Indic, Chinese or Islamic political thought and their linkages to these broader traditions which have in due time informed international relations discipline.

However, this gap has been filled by Adam Watson who in *The Evolution of International Society* has deliberated on the nature of ancient state systems. While the idea of order in ancient state systems is far from the conceptualisation of international society, there are two broad trends, which have been identified. These are: (a) hegemonial authority and (b) autonomy.

Hegemonial authority has been defined as extending to the whole system, where the system became a society within the compass of a common or dominant culture. The *mandala* theory of Kautilya fits appropriately into the system, encompassing society of states. Autonomy, according to Watson, was also an important factor in the Kautilyan conception of international system (society of states), where it was required by the conqueror to respect local forms and traditions. Watson also highlights that, according to the Kautilyan understanding, acceptance of autonomy could bring benefits to both the ruler and ruled, and that the enforcement of direct administration could require more effort, money and even more blood than it worth.[16] Thus, the idea of hegemony (dominance) but also autonomy of states has a legitimate place in the system of states conceptualised by Kautilya.

Order, thus, in the Kautilyan context, can be understood through the *mandala* theory at the international level and the concept of *dharma* and its interplay with *karma* at the societal (domestic) level. With the combination of these two important but distinct levels, order in the *Arthasastra* can be broadly understood through three parameters. These are institutions, agents and structures—which can also be termed as the essential operative principles of order. By institutions are meant the theoretical pillars of foreign policy, which are the six methods as enunciated by Kautilya. These six methods primarily can be associated with the augmentation of power and influence, diplomatic outmanoeuvring of the enemy, formation of allies, war being used as the last resort and relevance and significance of following just behaviour. These methods are indicative of an ordering principle because they are prescriptions on holding the state and disciplining of behaviour. The second ordering principle is agents which are primarily the states. The states, as mentioned above, were guided by *dharma*, whereby the king was supposed to follow certain codes of conduct. The *saptanga* models were the core pillars defining the capacity of the state as well as enabling it to enforce and implement decisions. The fulcrum of state action was *yogakshema*, whereby the welfare of the population was one of the central nodal points for state action. The third principle was structures and this broadly relates with the *mandala* theory. The *mandala* theory indicates that the capacity of the state was important as the dominant state was often the *vijigisu* (referred above).Thus, the Kautilyan understanding of order indicates that instead of anarchy or systemic factors shaping the international system, it was the capacity of the state which endowed order to the system.

Power

The concept of power (*balamsaktih*) has also been conceptualised in Western discourses and in its varied interpretations has been associated with influence, authority, violence and obedience to different degrees. In the *Arthasastra*, Kautilya elucidates the concept of power as a diplomatic tool to achieve political ends. He writes, "Strength is power; happiness is the objective of using power." There are certain interesting parallels which can be made with the notion of power, as it is broadly understood amongst political theorists. However, it needs to be noted that Kautilya seems to have referred to only *balamsaktihsukhamsiddhih* (happiness is success), Kangle translates this as "Success is (obtaining) happiness."

Legitimacy: Max Weber's understanding of power can be likened to his understanding of power as domination, where domination is the exercise of power through command and the probability that such command will be obeyed. Weber also believed that when legitimacy is ascribed by participants, power can be endured and sustained over a period of time. Weber also termed power as legitimate power. Weber took this analysis further to describe the state as the actor, who has the monopoly over the use of legitimate force. The idea of legitimacy on the use of legitimate-force can be equated with the *danda* being subsumed within the broader concept of *dharma*. *Danda*, in other words, was necessary to provide order to society. According to the *Arthasastra*, every society needs a sovereign power wielding *kshatra*, 'power of command', to maintain order and 'protect creatures'. Hence *dandaniti*, 'the science of punishment,' has been the core of the instruction of kings in ancient times.[17]

Soft and Hard Power: While Kautilya does not exclude the possibility of coercion, as is evident through the famous tactics of *sama, dana, bheda, danda,* power according to Kautilya is not just coercive power. He writes the three constituents of power are counsel and correct judgement, might i.e. the actual strength of the fighting forces; and enthusiasm and energy. He writes that the three are not equally important. Sheer military strength is more important than enthusiasm and power of judgement is superior to might.[18] He further writes "power is of three kinds; so is the success resulting from its use. Intellectual strength provides the power of good counsel; a prosperous treasury and a strong army provide physical power and valour is the basis of moral and energetic action. The success resulting from each one is intellectual, physical and psychological."

Authority: Hannah Arendt distinguishes authority from power and violence. Authority, according to Hannah Arendt, is incompatible with persuasion, which presupposes equality and works through a process of argumentation. Against the egalitarian order of persuasion stands the authoritarian order, which is always hierarchical. If authority is to be defined, it has to be in contradistinction to coercion and persuasion. The concept of authority in the Kautilyan society is very much visible through the deep penetration of the state in the society, especially in the economic realm. The reason for it differs from the totalitarian form of government is that the king does not rule as per his own whims and fancies, but is accountable to the population at large. In fact, some political thinkers have distinguished between authority and power. Authority implies an *adhikaar.* According to Bhikhu Parekh, "*Adhikaar* is a complex and difficult Hindu concept, as it meant a deserved right. A right one deserves to possess as judged by established social norms. A ruler thus acquired *adhikaar* to power when he was judged to possess appropriate intellectual and moral qualifications."[19]

Given these various shades of power in Kaultilyan *Arthasastra*, where do we place his understanding of power? While many would translate Kautilyan interpretation of power as an expansionist and coercive instrument, the reading of the text reflects that the idea of power lay at the distinct intersection of authority, legitimacy and soft/hard power. Power for Kautilya thus has a more of an authoritarian connotation and is broadly linked with the idea of the strengthening the role of state. One can even say that power as a conceptual category facilitated the idea of a strong state.

III. Conclusion

Thus, given the above analysis, it can be concluded that while there is some similarity between the concepts as understood in the *Arthasastra* and in the general Western understanding, there are, however, distinct strands in the *Arthasastra*, which require attention. The idea of political virtue or political morality comes out distinctly as one compares the key concepts of order and power. Political virtue defined as *dharma*, is a shared norm of just behaviour, which has given coherence and predictability to people's life—be it the king, ministers or the general public.[20] Another factor, which needs to be reckoned with, is the concept of state. Given that the state was the nodal point of analysis, the *Arthasastra* is relevant to the 21st century as it underlines the significance of a strong state. This is particularly so as the contemporary state is witnessing multi-fold challenges from the domestic front. The idea of state being an autonomous actor, prioritising domestic issues over external ones, is again a pointer towards strengthening state capacity and enhancing internal security.

This is particularly so, given the rise of Asia and the ongoing debate on the nature of changing power equations (economic, political and military) between countries, with many scholars arguing that the power shift from the West to the East is inevitable in the coming years. While the debate has been animated by scholars such as Kishore Mahbubani, G. John Ikenberry, Parag Khanna, John Mearsheimer, Fareed Zakaria and Charles Kupchan, it needs to be highlighted here that unless state capacity is improved and internal security issues are taken care of, the shift from the West to the East could be jeopardised by intra and internecine state conflicts. Kautilya's *Arthasastra*, therefore, becomes useful in understanding the nature of the state and in understanding the nature of geo-political clout at the international level, which itself stems from the internal wellbeing of the state.

NOTES

1. Shogo Suzuki, Yongjin Zjang and Joel Quirk critiquing the absence of non-western norms argue that international and cosmopolitan norms shared amongst humankind originate in the West and that non-Europeans hardly play a role in the production of international norms and they are nothing but takers of norms. For further details see: Shogo Suzuki and Yongjin, *International Orders in the Early Modern World: Before the Rise of the West,* Routledge, New York, 2014.
2. B.P. Sinha, for instance, defines it as a welfare state as he argues that the state interest was primarily an extension of the interest of the people and that there was no difference between the sovereign authority and that of the people. He highlights the positive role played by the state, primarily in the economic and social sphere.
3. L.N. Rangarajan, *Kautilya: The Arthashastra,* Penguin Books, London, 1987, p. 43.
4. *Ibid.*, p. 167.
5. *Ibid.*, p. 20.
6. *Ibid.*
7. *Ibid.*, p. 224.
8. B.K. Sarkar, "Hindu Theory of International Relations", *The American Political Science Review,* 13(3), August 1919, pp. 405-406.
9. Benno Teschke, *The Myth of 1648: Class, Geo Politics and the Making of Modern International Relations*, Verso, New York, 2003, p. 7.
10. L.N. Rangarajan, *Kautilya: The Arthashastra,* Penguin Books, London, 1987, p. 133.
11. *Ibid.*, p. 156.
12. B.P. Sinha, *Readings in Arthashastra,* Agam Prakashan, Delhi, 1971, p. 11.
13. Hedley Bull, *The Anarchical Society: The Study of Order in World Politics,* Palgrave Macmillan, New York, 1977, pp. 3-4.
14. *Ibid.*, p. 53.
15. *Ibid.*, pp. 170-172.
16. Adam Watson, *The Evolution of International Society: A Comparative Historical Analysis,* Routledge, New York, 1992, p. 124.
17. Gurcharan Das, *India Grows at Night: The Liberal Case for a Strong State*, Penguin Books, Delhi, 2013, p. 92.
18. L.N. Rangarajan, *Kautilya: The Arthashastra,* Penguin Books, London, 1987, p. 588.
19. Bhikhu Parekh, "Some Reflection on Hindu Tradition of Political Thought", in Fred Dallmayr, *Comparative Political Theory: An Introduction,* Palgrave Macmillan, New York, 2010, p. 112.
20. Gurcharan Das, note 17, p. 92.

3

Exploring the Concepts of Grand Strategy and Strategic Planning in Kautilya's *Arthaśāstra* through a Hermeneutical Lens

G. Adityakiran

Kautilya's *Arthaśāstra* is a compendium of instructions for a king (leadership) about statecraft and the governance of a state. It was not meant for the ordinary citizenry but was a detailed manual only meant for the king. It dealt with the science of acquisition and preservation of territory of a state in order to ensure the developed life and security of its citizens. About two thousand four hundred years ago, Kautilya compiled the *Arthaśāstra* which has endured the test of time and credibility. When a profound thinker as him, demonstrates vision and foresight, it is useful to understand the elements of this thought construct that could have applicability in contemporary times. Learning and grasping even a fraction of the wisdom that Kautilya embodied in his treatise, would enrich policy makers today. It is a treatise that encapsulates in many ways the complexity of the present. The problems that existed then, persist in a more widespread and convoluted manner in today's world.

The *Arthaśāstra* contains a total of fifteen books (*adhikaranas*). Of these, the first five deal with the internal administration of the state (*tantra*) while the next eight delve into its relations with neighbouring states (*āvāpa*).[1] This indicates that foreign affairs were a very important aspect of Kautilya's *Arthaśāstra* which has not been replicated in other Indian texts of that era. The cornerstone of his thesis is that the king needs to aspire to be a would-be-conqueror (*vijigisu*)[2] in order to usher in progress and happiness within his kingdom and also increase his power compared to his neighbours. The lawfully ruled state was necessary for civilised society, and without it, there would be anarchy and lawlessness. In order to replace the rule of 'unbridled might' (which could result in 'law of fishes'[3]) with the rule of 'right', the establishment of societal order was a felt necessity. Therefore, the king, and thereby the state, was said to have three main objectives. The first objective was to maintain and preserve societal order (*loksangraha*). The second objective was to stimulate growth by acquisition in order to make the state prosperous as also create conditions for the populace to enjoy its fruits (*yogakshema*). The third objective was to secure socio-economic progress of its citizens (*labhpalana*). With these three goals in focus, Kautilya exhorted the king to expand his kingdom.

This paper aims to explore the *Arthaśāstra* to cull out Kautilya's concept of Grand Strategy as he exhorts the *vijigisu* to expand his state's power in order to achieve the objectives of *yogakshema* and *labhpalana* while ensuring *loksangraha*. This paper is based on a qualitative research methodology called hermeneutics. It etymologically relates to the Greek god Hermes in his role as the interpreter of the messages of the gods. In the current context, hermeneutics could be described as the interpretation and understanding of ancient literatures and religious texts. It is also used in contemporary philosophy to denote the study of theories and methods of the interpretation of all texts and systems of meaning.[4] In this paper, a few aphorisms of the *Arthaśāstra* would be delved deeper and interpreted within the modern day context, in order to identify and explore the nuances of grand strategy and strategic planning.

What is Grand Strategy?

The word strategy means the art of command of a general and is a predominantly military lexicon. It has now crept into modern management usage and has lost its essential meaning.[5] In the early 1940s, Edward Earle expanded the concept of strategy beyond war to include activity in peacetime. He stated that strategy required increasing consideration of other national non-military factors—economic, psychological, moral, political and technological—and was the art of controlling all the resources of a nation in order to effectively promote and secure its vital interests against actual or potential enemies. Moreover, in Earle's view, grand strategy integrated policies and military efforts of a nation in such a manner that resorting to war is either rendered unnecessary or was undertaken with the maximum likelihood of victory. Earle thus interpreted 'grand strategy' as applicable in both peace and war. However, both applications were war-oriented, since it was war as the subject of grand strategy which had to be either prevented, or prepared for, in peacetime.[6]

A 'grand' strategy entails the broadest conception of how an objective is to be attained. It serves to coordinate and direct all available resources (human, economic, political, moral, spiritual, etc.) to attain its objectives. Grand strategy essentially straddles a broad spectrum of national capabilities including, but not limited to, those provided by the military and links them to policy objectives. Policy represents a choice leading to a course of action proposed or adopted by a government. It is a statement of intent, or a commitment to act. Policy decisions provide strategy makers with the objectives or 'ends' to which they must ascribe 'ways' and 'means'. Strategy is not policy, but the ways and means of making it reality. Policy could be aspirational, but good policy must be grounded in a realistic framework of national influence and capabilities—the 'ways and means' elements of strategy.[7]

The concept of grand strategy can be reduced to three basic elements: First, its statement of intentional practice forged in a specific context; second, a strategy which is executed by leaders; third, a strategy which is influenced and altered by the actions of enemies no less than one's own goals.[8] The essential goal of a political strategy is war. "Regardless of the specific methods used, war has been and is still about the use of armed forces to achieve specific political purposes, although the means and methods change."[9] The strategy of planning and orchestrating war covers a much broader scope than warfare, since the former also includes the struggle on the non-military fronts. Strategy as the theory and practice of preparing a country and its armed forces for war is an activity carried out in peacetime, and thus constitutes a significant part of state activity.[10]

Therefore, grand strategy is a future centric discipline. That is its objective. Grand strategy has to be predictable for it to have relevance. What contributes primarily to this predictability is the 'means' or the resources which define the quantum of futuristic action possible. It is always the means which gives a predictability and timeline of achieving the 'end'. While stated policy goals or 'ends' determine the desired aspirational aim, the 'ways' determine if the chosen grand strategy is better than the adversary's.[11] Arthur Lykke Jr. has succinctly described the 'ends–ways–means' framework:

> "'Ends' can be expressed as military objectives and 'Ways' are concerned with the various methods of applying military force. In essence, this becomes an examination of courses of action that are designed to achieve the military objective. 'Means' refers to the military resources (manpower, material, money, forces, logistics etc.) required to accomplish the mission."[12]

Objectives laid out in the *Arthaśāstra*

The *Arthaśāstra* sets before the *vijigisu* the goal of conquest of the world (*chakravartin*) and describes ways of achieving it while ensuring the triad of *yogakshema, labhpalana* and *loksangraha*. The policy objectives or 'ends' identified by Kautilya are therefore threefold. They are:

1. Promoting economic progress
2. Ensuring national security in order to enjoy the fruits of economic progress
3. Preserving societal order

The Kautilyan state was predominantly agrarian in nature. The state sustained by the revenue it collected from its citizens who followed various professions/vocations and paid taxes to the state. The three main vocations which provided livelihood and hence taxes to the state were agriculture (*krishi*), cattle rearing (*pashupalya*) and trade (*vanijya*). These three vocations together constituted *vartta* (economy).[13] These provided grains, cattle, money, forest produce and labour to the state.

All industry related to agriculture, mining, forestry, cattle-rearing and commodity trading was seen as the primary source of revenue. It sustained the treasury (*kosa*) and the army (*danda*) which made it possible for the state to provide for its people as well as keep its enemies in check. To develop the agrarian economy it was essential to settle in newer lands (*shunyanivesha*). Therefore, it was imperative for an agrarian state to expand its territories. It was the duty of the state to create conditions that could allow its citizens to earn their livelihood honestly while expanding their agricultural lands and enjoy the fruits of their hard labour in peace.[14] Since it was a monarch who ruled the state, the qualities he needed to display for effective leadership and for formulating the state's policy objectives were covered and expounded in great detail in the *Arthaśāstra*.

Herein lies the relevance of studying the *Arthaśāstra* as it demonstrates that the political leadership, governance, policy formulation, policy execution and progress—all these had to be linked to the welfare of the people. One of the core themes of Kautilya's *Arthaśāstra* is that it exposits a relation between governance and economic progress with political stability. While the state's goal was economic progress alongside political stability, governance was a means towards achieving that goal. Good governance was intrinsic to the Kautilyan concept of administration and was therefore inextricably linked to protecting the social order of the polity. Kautilya based the development of the state on stimulating and encouraging economic growth. Therefore, one of his major contributions is his pioneering theory of economic growth which even today has no parallel in its range and entirety.[15]

Doctrine of *Prakritis*

Having laid down clearly the foremost aim of the *vijigisu*, Kautilya proceeded to expound on the doctrine of *prakritis*[16] or the seven organic elements of a state.[17] These are the king (*swamin*), the group of ministers and officials (*amatya*), the natural resources, territory and skilled populace of the state (*janapada*), fortified towns (*durg*), the treasury (*kosa*), the military forces (*danda/bala*) and the allies (*mitra*). It is interesting to note that while the *Arthaśāstra* text subsequently[18] includes the enemy leadership in the *prakritis*' elaboration, the first verse of Chapter Six,[19] where the *prakritis* are first mentioned, does not. This is interesting because, for the first time, the nature of the enemy and his qualities, have been included in detailing the resources of a state. This would help in planning considerations and determining the adversary to attack.

Swami is the term used to denote the sovereign ruler. It refers to sovereigns in both monarchical and republic states. In elaborating on the calamities affecting the ruler, Kautilya mentions the weakness of *vairajya*, a non-monarchical state.[20] The intention is to stress that the *swami* holds an exalted position in a Kautilyan state. *Amatya* refers to the bureaucrats, administration and judiciary. Since they actually administer the state, their importance is next to the sovereign ruler. *Janapada* refers to the countryside and its populace. *Durg* refers to the fortified towns and its infrastructure while *kosa* refers to the treasury of the state without which *danda*, the army, cannot be maintained.

Danda/bala is the fundamental cornerstone of the Kautilyan state and provides the ruler with ability to rule justly. The ruler, it has been emphasised, also derives his power from the devotion and allegiance of the populace. He is, therefore, advised to see no interest other than the interest of his subjects and to guard against their dissatisfaction.[21] Kautilya declares that a ruler endowed of personal excellences, as also that of the other *prakritis*, can be termed as a *vijigisu*, provided that he has an excellent grasp of policy and strategy (*nayasyadhishtanam*).[22] Expansion of the *janapada* was the predominant duty of the *vijigisu*. This could be carried out by attacking the neighbouring state and annexing its territory. This would result in more finances which in turn could strengthen the state and make it more powerful to expand further. The *prakritis* were vital to the nation-state and contributed to its national power in the same order as given. It was therefore incumbent on a state to weaken the *prakritis* of the adversary in the same order whilst strategising an attack.

The theory of *prakritis* is popularly known as the *saptanga* theory of sovereignty of a nation-state which is also mentioned in the *Manusmriti* and the *Shanti Parva* of the *Mahabharata*. The term *saptanga* means seven-limbed. It means that the nation-state is seen as an organic whole having seven limbs. Just as a human body is meant to be most productive and happy when healthy, so too, a nation-state is said to be prosperous and successful when all its organs/elements are healthy and strong. Just as a body weakens and is susceptible to pain and distress when any of its organs is afflicted by disease, so too, a nation-state would be weakened when any of its elements/organs sustains a calamity (*vyasana*).

The Means

This characterisation is important to understand the ephemeral and evolving nature of a nation-state's foreign affairs. A strong nation-state over a period of time will degenerate to a weaker nation-state with passage of time, as leadership evolves and also other elements of the state are not as productive as earlier once they start enjoying the fruits of their labour and then get afflicted due to one or the other calamity befalling them (in a similar fashion to a healthy body weakening due to lack of exercise). *Prakritis* are, therefore, the 'means', the resources which would be utilised to achieve the nation's stated objectives.

Sadgunya: The Six Courses of Action of Foreign Policy

Kautilya enunciates six courses of action of foreign policy.[23] However, these were not originated by Kautilya. These have been part and parcel of ancient Indian lore and have been extensively elaborated in the *Mahabharata*.[24] These are:

(a) *Samdhi*—making peace
(b) *Vigraha*—initiating hostile action
(c) *Asana*—staying quiet
(d) *Yana*—marching
(e) *Samsraya*—seeking protection
(f) *Dvaidhibhava*—Dual policy of making peace with one to pursue a policy of hostility to another.[25]

The general rule being that when one is weaker than the adversary, *samdhi* is the policy to be followed; if stronger than him then *vigraha*. If both are equal in power, *asana* is the right policy; but if one is very strong *yana* could be resorted to. When one is very weak, *samsraya* is necessary; while *dvaidhibhava* is the policy recommended when with help from another source one can fight one's adversary. The purpose of all policies is that the conqueror should increase his power in the longer run, principally at the adversary's cost, though sometimes he may have to tolerate temporarily the greater strength of the adversary.[26] This is preliminary to the realisation of conquering the world (*chakravartin*). The adoption of one or the other of the six policies is to be solely guided by this supreme criterion of self-interest. Thus, the appropriate use of the *sadgunya* would enable the conqueror (*vijigisu*) to manipulate other kings as he pleases and they become tied to him by virtue of his intellectual prowess.[27]

The choice of an appropriate course of action is dependent on the strength of the individual *prakritis* of the adversary against whom it is directed. Kautilya analyses this thoroughly in great detail and suggests appropriate measures using the *sadgunya.* All these measures have one basic principle underlying them, i.e. to weaken the elements (*prakritis*) of the adversary state while simultaneously strengthening his own.

By projecting power using an appropriate course of action in foreign policy of the *sadgunya*, the king is successful and makes progress, thus contributing to intensifying his power. Therefore, a dynamic relationship between progress and power, mediated by the right foreign policy, exists between the states surrounding the *vijigisu's* state.[28] This application of a certain course of action of foreign policy to the neighbouring states was termed as the *Raja Mandala*, the Theory of Circle of Kings.

Raja Mandala Theory

Kautilya propounded and developed a unique theory of foreign policy aptly called the *Raja Mandala* or the *Circle of Kings*. This theory propounds that a country's immediate neighbours could be hostile adversaries, neutral or vassal states, while their neighbours would be natural allies of the said country. In other words, if the said nation state is in the centre, an immediate concentric circle would be adversarial or neutral, while the next concentric circle of nation states with contiguous boundaries to the adversaries would be its natural allies. The *Raja Mandala* is a complex grouping of nation states which in concentric circles would then be expanded to give the same relationships so on and so forth. To put it plainly, an adversary's adversary is your friend.

The terms given by Kautilya to the constituents of the *Raja Mandala* are *vijigisu* (conqueror), *ari* (adversary), *mitra* (ally), *ari-mitra* (adversary's ally), *mitra-mitra* (ally's ally), *parshnigraha* (adversary in the rear), *aakranda* (ally in the rear), *madhyama* ('middle king'), *udasina* ('neutral king').[29] The 'middle king', *madhyama,* is one with territory adjoining both the *vijigisu* and the *ari* and is powerful than either of them. The 'neutral king', *udasina*, is one whose borders are farther away but is a far more stronger and powerful than the 'middle king'. The *vijigisu* is to plan his conquests in different ways according to the circumstances prevailing at that point of time. There exist four possibilities which need to be considered and have been exposited by Kautilya.[30]

(a) When there is the regular *mandala*, the *vijigisu* should conquer the *ari*; with his strength thus augmented he must overcome the *madhyama*, the 'middle king'; thereafter he should take on the *udasina,* the 'neutral king'. Thus he establishes suzerainty over the *mandala*.
(b) When there is neither a *madhyama* nor an *udasina*, but only allies and adversaries exist, he should first try to subdue the adversaries after securing the allegiance of his allies.
(c) When there are only two other states, one hostile and the other friendly, he should try to squeeze and crush one of them between himself and the other; it is immaterial which state is crushed. Once that is achieved, the other state could be tackled accordingly.
(d) When the *vijigisu* is surrounded by a number of hostile neighbouring states, he should tackle them one at a time, growing in strength as he proceeds with his conquests.[31]

Upayas (Conflict Resolution Methods)

There are four basic conflict resolution methods laid out in the *Arthaśāstra* which are termed as *upayas*. These are *sama*—adopting a conciliatory attitude, *dana*—placating with rewards and gifts, *bheda*—sowing dissension amongst enemies and *danda*—using force. It is easier to employ a method earlier in order than the latter one. Placating with gifts is twice as hard as

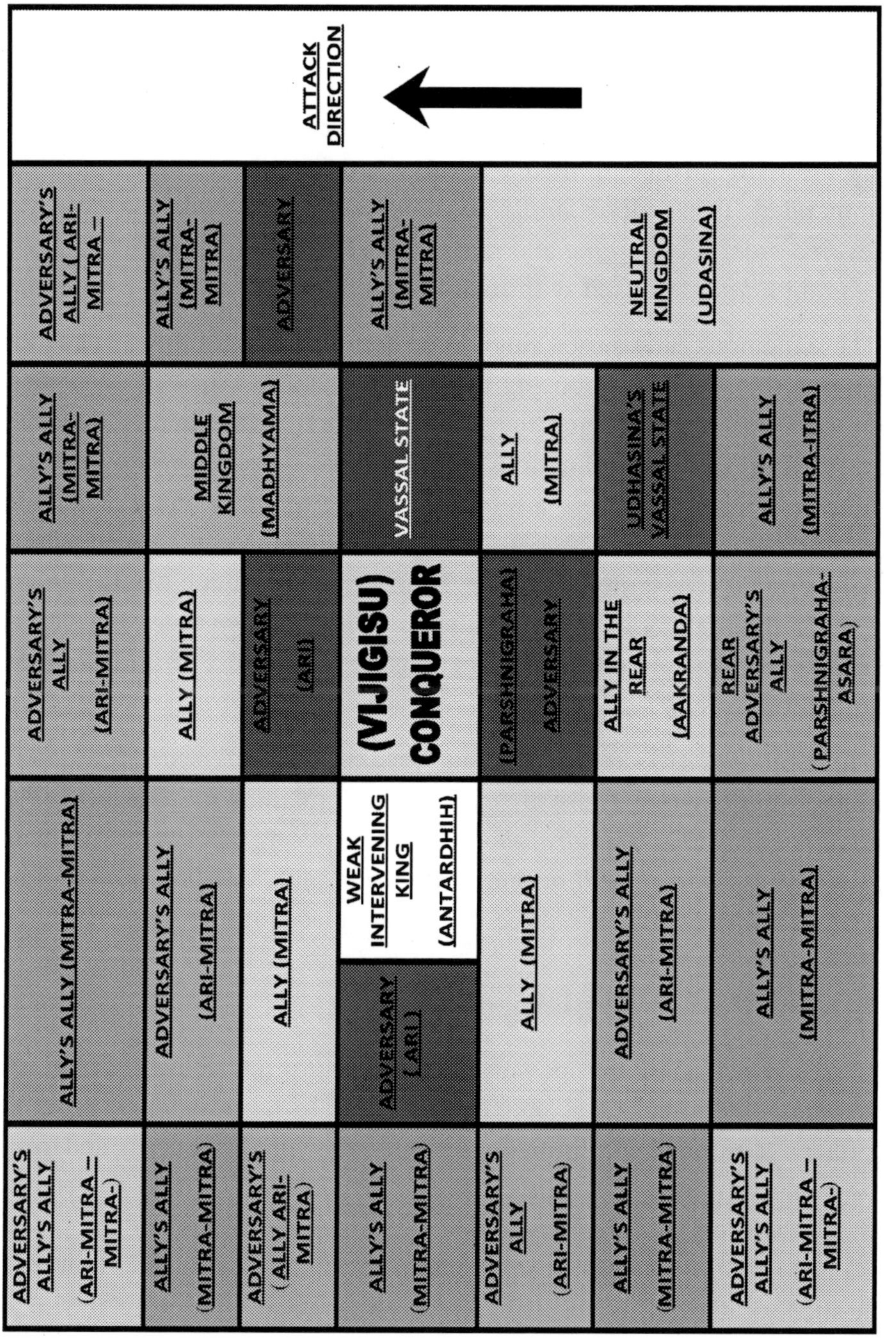

Fig. 1: The *Raja Mandala*: Circle of States

conciliation, sowing dissension three times as hard and use of force four times.[32] The recommended methods are that while dealing with next of kin, *sama and dana* are to be used. In case of placating the military or citizens of the state, then *dana and bheda* are the right methods. In case of a neighbouring prince or forest chiefs, use of *bheda and danda* is recommended. This order is *anuloma* (natural). If the methods are used in the reverse order, i.e. if *sama* and *dana* is used with neighbouring princes, if *bheda* and *danda* is used with own kith and kin, it is called *pratiloma.*

These methods can be used singly or in combination. Kautilya calculates fifteen possible ways of choosing these combinations when in one order. When the issue of employing the easier one first or the harder one first comes to fore, these combinations double; thus, these give rise to thirty possible combinations. There are four ways of using any one method, six ways of using any two at a time, four ways of using three at a time and one way of using all four simultaneously. Thus, there are fifteen ways of using these methods singly or in any combination in the *anuloma* order, the natural order. Likewise, there are fifteen ways of using them in the *pratiloma* order, the unnatural order.[33]

Three more *upayas* are included in the texts like *Shukraniti, Brihaspati Sutra* and *Agni Purana*. These are *upekshana* (remaining indifferent), *maya* (passive deception) and *aindrajala* (active deception). These are important whilst waging *kutayuddha*, *gudhayuddha* and *tusnimyuddha*. The *Arthaśāstra* alludes to these three in various places in the text.

Nature of Power Explained

The *Arthaśāstra* states that power and success are interrelated. There are three *shaktis* or powers that operate in a state in the ascending order of importance. *Utsahashakti*, (individual power) the personal energy and drive of the leadership as well as the citizenry; *prabhushakti*, (hard power) the power of the army and treasury and *mantrashakti* (soft power), the power of counsel and diplomacy. The application of power would lead to success. Such success as that as resulting from each one is therefore intrinsic, physical and diplomatic. These powers are only thought of in connection with a state's relations with other states and have no bearing on the internal structure of a state's organisation.

Before planning a war or a foreign policy initiative, the *vijigisu* must satisfy himself that he has measured the power of his state. He needs to ensure that the state is superior in three respects. These are, the three powers (*shaktis*), the terrain (*desa*) in which the fight is likely to take place and the season *(kala)* when fighting may be expected. Kautilya opines that these are mutually helpful and are, therefore, of equal importance.[34] With wise counsel and clever diplomacy, a king can easily overcome energetic or mighty rivals.[35] This brings out clearly the importance of the diplomatic and intellectual power (soft power)[36] over military power (hard power). The above could be tabulated thus:[37]

No.	Strength	Power	Success
a	Intellectual and Moral Strength	Good Counsel and Diplomacy (*Mantrashakti*) (***Soft Power***)	Diplomatic (*Mantrasiddhih*)
b	Economic and Military Strength	Physical Power (*Prabhushakti*) (***Hard Power***)	Physical (*Prabhusiddhih*)
c	Courage and Valour of the King and Populace	Energetic Power (*Utsahashakti*) (***Individual Power***)	Intrinsic (*Utsahasiddhih*)

Hence, soft power, hard power, individual power, terrain and the weather, all play an equal importance and need to be taken into consideration before making any strategic policy moves over an adversary. This measured and quantitative comparison would help unravel the relative balance of power equation between the adversary and the conqueror and would help in selecting the correct course of action to be adopted.

Kautilya emphasises that it is soft power that lays the foundation of an effective and active foreign policy. However, in order to effectively and completely overpower any adversary, the conqueror needs to focus on beefing up the state's soft, hard and individual powers. Kautilya's unique application of the *Raja Mandala Theory* is unprecedented in its clarity of thought and applicability even today. Moreover, he discusses the need to have more focus on soft power as compared to hard power.[38] He stresses the success of a foreign policy does not depend purely on military power (hard power) but more on the intellectual power and moral power (soft power).[39]

Types of Wars: 'The Ways'

To achieve his objectives, the ruler will use his resources, the *prakritis*, to wage five kinds of war which would utilise the *sadgunya* and the *upayas*. This is a significant contribution of the *Arthaśāstra* as Kautilya puts forth how to conduct war even under peaceful conditions in the state. The five kinds of war are:

(a) *Prakashayuddha* (Open War)[40]—This war is openly waged and is fought on the lines of *dharmayuddha*. It is fought with rules and within a lawful framework and is a conventional war in modern lexicon. Wars between two nations like India-Pakistan wars of 1965, 1971 and the World Wars fall in this category.

(b) *Kutayuddha* (Deception War)[40]—This war is fought on exactly opposite terms of *dharmayuddha*. It is an unrighteous and deceitful war fought with no restrictions and in which time-honoured principles are sacrificed at the altar of expediency. *Kutayuddha* permits the use of deadly and poisonous weapons which can cause mass destruction and slay thousands of persons. The objective is paramount and no means are restricted from achieving it whether legal or illegal. The shunned methods of conflict resolution like *maya* (passive deception) and *aindrajala* (active deception) are used in *kutayuddha*. It was recommended to be carried out against the wicked and the seditious. A modern-day example of this kind of warfare would be the terrorist groups which wage war against states and do not hesitate to murder innocents to further their agenda.

(c) *Tusnimyuddha* (Silent War)[40]—This war is in sharp contrast to the previous two types of wars. In this war, the enemy is struck silently in order to not draw public attention to the doer. However, the objective is always paramount. This form of warfare was conducted when the opponent was a stronger state and *sandhi* or *asana* were the forms of *sadgunya* being practiced between both the states. Cyber Warfare is a form of *tusnimyuddha*.

(d) *Mantrayuddha* (Diplomatic War)[41]—This involves a battle of intrigue and also by giving wrongful counsel. It involves spreading rumours, falsehood, applying threats of public shame and loss of face which compel the state leadership to toe the line dictated. It does not involve loss of human life or capital. It is followed when the state wishes to avoid war and uses soft power to deny the adversary the advantage or the opportunity to wage war against it. Examples of *mantrayuddha* include use of international institutions like IMF / World Bank / NPT to apply pressure on a nation and use of United Nations (UN) sanctions to force a country to toe the international opinion.

(e) *Gudhayuddha* (Secret War)[42]—It employs covert violence to confound and subvert the enemy while assassinating the enemy's leadership and important infrastructure. An example of *gudhayuddha* is a state employing irregulars to disrupt the progress of the adversary while outwardly it enjoys regular diplomatic ties with it. While *kutayuddha* implies initiating the foreign policy of *vigraha, gudhayuddha* means the nation does not openly profess adopting *vigraha.* Hence, it is a secret war which is subterranean, lurking below the false premise of good and excellent foreign relations existing between the two nations.

Therefore, the grand strategy which Kautilya unravelled for a *vijigisu* was different for a different adversary. He intended that the ruler use the *prakritis* (Means in Lykke's model), after determining the exact relative power disparity, and decide on the type of war using the appropriate

Fig. 2: The Framework of Grand Strategy

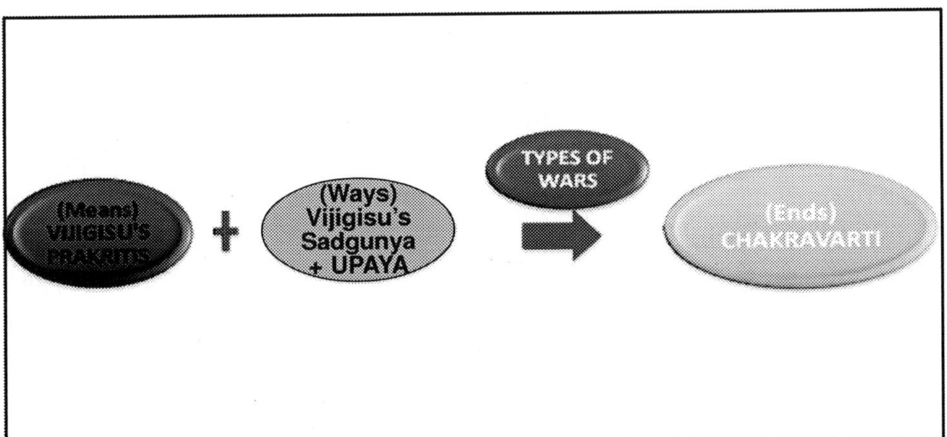

combination of the *sadgunya* and *upaya* ('Ways' in Lykke's Model) so as to achieve the national objectives ('Ends' in Lykke's Model).

Planning of a Campaign

Kautilya lists eight different factors which must be taken into consideration before deciding to proceed on a campaign. These are in the order of importance: power (diplomatic, military and individual), place of operations, time, kind of mobilised troops, time of season, nature of gains to be achieved, extent of losses possible and possibility of treachery. The modern factors of force, space and time have been thus taken into consideration in addition to five more factors which, according to Kautilya, have a lot of importance in planning a campaign. These have been given specific weightage and accordingly measured qualitatively and quantitatively. The decision thereafter is taken whether or not to wage a campaign.[43] Strategic planning lets you think through all possible contingencies in advance so as to make fewer tactical errors while executing it. But a ruler, who makes the fewest errors by thinking through various contingencies and who has adequately prepared, organised and trained his *prakritis*, always wins.

Conclusion

Kautilya was a realist strategist positing that states need to be self-interested, power-seeking rational actors, seeking to maximise their security and chances of survival beyond the natural time-cycle of a nation's longevity. The *Arthaśāstra* explains the theories of neo-realism or structural realism whilst a *vijigisu* aspires to become a sole strong power (*chakravartin*). It also explains the failure of the theory of structural realism once a unipolar world comes into being. However, it is not the case, as delving deeper into the *prakriti* theory, it can be understood that states too like human bodies, are subject to afflictions, illnesses and degeneration (*vyasana*) with passage of time. This would lead the state to improve its elements and sue for peace with its neighbours. It also explains the reluctance of an afflicted state to wage war in an anarchic system of states and sue for peace by increasing inter-dependence amongst the immediate neighbours, whereby displaying liberal intent. Grand Strategy as a future-centric discipline has been explored and dissected into its constituent elements and re-assembled to illuminate a framework which is universally applicable irrespective of the nation-state in question.

Kautilya's *Arthaśāstra* is one of the ancient Indian literatures which had provided some insights to strategy, although it was written for kings to govern the state. The theory of grand strategy as posited in the *Arthaśāstra* exemplifies the clarity of thought, purpose and tenacity essential in a strategist in order to achieve the aims or goals of the nation-state. The framework of the *prakriti* (ways) and *sadgunya* and *upaya* (means) to achieve the given aim whilst utilising the various types of war, is a pioneering and articulate contribution to the thought of grand strategy. There are many concepts of strategy from Kautilya's *Arthaśāstra*, which are still applicable in a nation-state's strategic security calculus within its neighbourhood. A deeper study of the book will open many new areas of International Relations concepts, which are yet to be known and practised in the modern foreign policy by experts and practitioners.

NOTES

1. R.P. Kangle, *The Kautiliya Arthasastra Part III* (2nd ed.), Bombay University Press, Mumbai, 1969, p. 19.
2. R.P. Kangle, *The Kautiliya Arthasastra Part II* (2nd ed.), Bombay University Press, Mumbai, 1969, p. 318, [6.2.13].
3. R.P. Kangle, *The Kautiliya Arthasastra Part I* (2nd ed), Bombay University Press, Mumbai, 1969, p. 6, [1.4.13].
   "*Apranitastu matsyanyayam udbhavayati*—If not used rightly, it gives rise to the law of fishes." According to the law of fishes, the bigger fish swallows the smaller fish and thus is established a situation similar to law of the jungle. It means that if you remove laws and rules to govern justly, society will fall into anarchy where the strong dominates the weak, where one has to survive using strength or cunning and where might is right.
4. Michael N. Forster, "Hermeneutics", in Brian Leiter & Michael Rosen (eds.), *The Oxford Handbook of Continental Philosophy,* Oxford University Press, Oxford, 2007, available at http://philosophy.uchicago.edu/faculty/files/forster/HERM.pdf.
5. Strategy has its etymological basis in the French word "*stratégie*" meaning "art of a general", which has its roots in the Greek word "*strategia*" meaning "office or command of a general."
6. Edward Mead Earle, *The Makers of Modern Strategy*, Princeton University Press, Princeton, 1944, pp. vii-viii.
7. "Organising Defence's Contribution to National Strategy", Paper by Defence Strategy

Group, MoD, UK, available at http://www.da.mod.uk/recommended-reading/organisation/documents/85_20121116-Organising_Defences_contribution_to_National_Strategy-U.pdf .

8. Irving Louis Horowitz, "Relativists and Absolutists: Grand Strategies in a World of Fractured Norms," *Society*, 50(1), 2013, pp. 48-54.
9. John Andreas Olsen and Colin S. Gray, *The Practice of Strategy: From Alexander the Great to the Present,* Oxford University Press, New York & Oxford, 2011. pp. 287–300.
10. J. Lider, "Towards a Modern Concept of Strategy," *Cooperation and Conflict*, XVI, 1981, pp. 217-235, available at http://cac.sagepub.com/content/16/4/217.
11. Lukas Milevski, "Whence Derives Predictability in Strategy", *Infinity Journal*, 2(4), Fall 2012, pp. 4-7.
12. Arthur F. Lykke, Jr., "Toward an Understanding of Military Strategy," in Joseph R. Cerami and James F. Holcomb, Jr. (eds.), *US Army War College Guide to Strategy*, Strategic Studies Institute, Carlisle, 2001, p. 180.
13. R.P. Kangle, note 2, p. 9, [1.4.1-2].
14. *Ibid.*, p. 317, [6.2.1-3]. "*Shama vyayamau yogakshemayoh yonih. Karma arambhanam yogaaradhano vyayamah. Karmaphala upabhoganam kshemaradhanah shamah.*" Peace and industry constitute the source of acquisition and security. Industry is that which brings about accomplishment of the undertaken works. Absence of disturbance to the enjoyment of the results achieved from works is peace.
15. Marinko Škare, "The Missing Link: From Kautilya's the Arthashastra to Modern Economics", *The Journal of Philosophical Economics*, VI(2) 2013. Also William H. McNeill and Jean W. Sedlar (eds.), *Classical India*, Oxford University Press, New York, 1969, pp. 20-22.
16. R.P. Kangle, note 1, p. 127.
17. L.N. Rangarajan, *Kautilya: The Arthashastra*, Penguin Classics, Delhi, 1992, p. 97.
18. R.P. Kangle, note 3, p. 165, [6.1.13-15].
19. *Ibid.*, p. 164, [6.1.1].
20. *Ibid.*, p. 207, [8.2.5].
21. *Ibid.*, p. 27, [1.19.36]. "*Praja sukhe sukham rajnyaha prajanam cha hite hitam. Natma priyam hitam rajnyaha prajanam tu priyam hitam.*" Meaning: "In the happiness of his public rests the king's happiness, in their welfare his welfare. He shall not consider as good only that which pleases him but treat as beneficial to him whatever pleases his public."
22. *Ibid.*, p. 165, [6.2.13].
23. L.N. Rangarajan, note 17, p. 512.
24. *Vidura Niti*, Chapter 1, *sutra* 43 (English Translation by K.M. Ganguli).
Meaning: Discriminating the two (what is to be done and what is not to be done) by means of the one (the intellect), bring under thy subjection the three (friend, enemy and the neutral person) by means of four (the four means of success against an enemy—*sama*, reconciliation or negotiation; *dana*, bribery; *bheda*, sowing dissensions and *danda*, punishment), and also conquering the five (senses of perception) and knowing the six (six expedients to be used in foreign politics—*sandhi, vigraha, yana,*

asana, dvaidhibhava and samshraya) and abstaining from the seven (woman, gambling, hunting, intoxicants, harsh speech, harsh punishment and amassing wealth using unjust means), be happy.

25. L.N. Rangarajan, note 17, pp. 512-514.
26. R.P. Kangle, note 1, p. 251.
27. *Ibid.*, p. 255.
28. L.N. Rangarajan, note 17, p. 517.
29. *Ibid.*, pp. 517-523.
30. R.P. Kangle, note 1, p. 256.
31. *Ibid.*, p. 257.
32. L.N. Rangarajan, note 17, p. 91.
33. *Ibid.*, p. 93.
34. R.P. Kangle, note 1, pp. 256-257.
35. *Ibid.* pp. 128-129.
36. Joseph S. Nye, Jr., "Soft Power", *Foreign Policy*, No. 80, Twentieth Anniversary, Fall 1990, p. 166.
37. L.N. Rangarajan, note 17, pp. 525-526.
38. Ibid., p. 525.
39. *Ibid.*, p. 517.
40. R.P. Kangle, note 3, p. 178, [7.6.17]. *Vikramasya prakashayuddham kutayuddham tushnimyuddham.*
41. *Ibid.*, p. 249, [12.1.17]. *Tesham anyatamam uthishthamaanam sandhina mantrayuddhena kutayuddhena va prativyuhet.*
42. *Ibid.*, p. 253, [12.4.24]. *Lubdhakvyanjana va vaskandasankuleshu gudhayuddha hetubhih abhihanyuh.*
43. L.N. Rangarajan, note 17, pp. 586-604.

PART II

ISSUES OF STRATEGY, ART AND LAWS OF WAR

4

Kautilya's *Arthasastra*: An Approach to Counter-Insurgency Strategy

Vinay Vittal

Kautilya's *Arthasastra* is one of the major political and strategic treatises that constitute a collection of timeless concepts. The *Arthasastra* is a guide for rulers to ensure protection of a state from external aggression, maintenance of law and order within the state, safeguarding the welfare of the people and promoting economic prosperity. Kautilya's *Arthasastra* provides guidance to a wise king to assist the leader in managing the state through transition from a state of decline to one of stabilisation, and from there to achieve progress or advancement. The policy to be employed depends on the relative power, strategic environment, and dynamics of the political situation. The *Arthasastra* is not a treatise based on general principles, but a strategy concerned with recommending practicable policies in any conceivable situation. Some of the strategies could be gainfully employed to achieve long-term benefits and resolve some of the key issues affecting numerous countries today that include insurgency. The power lies in true interpretation of the *Arthasastra* to unravel timeless grand strategy to achieve a better peace.

Insurgency

Insurgency has been defined by Kautilya as "calamities due to acts of men" wherein he states that most insurgencies are created by failed policies of the state. The United States Department of Defence defines insurgency as "An organized movement aimed at the overthrow of a constituted government through use of subversion and armed conflict." The major characteristic of the insurgency includes battle for control of the population. The support of the population is critical for the existence and advancement of insurgency.

Centrality of Population in Counter-Insurgent Strategy

According to Kautilya, the focus of statecraft should always be the safety and comfort of the people of the state—the word *artha* simply denotes the material wellbeing of the individuals.[1] Therefore, key to Kautilya's persuasiveness is that the *Arthasastra* emphasises the need for the formulation of a strategy to centre on the population. Consequently, it is evident that the counter-insurgency strategy has to be oriented towards the needs of the population. The duties of a king as stated by Kautilya include protection of the people of the state from external aggression; maintenance of law and order within the state; and safeguarding the economic welfare of the people.

Contemporary Counter-Insurgency Strategy

David Galula, the French military counter-insurgency strategist, propagated five basic principles of counter-insurgent warfare. The first principle stated that the objective is population. He explained that destruction of the rebel forces and occupation of the geographical terrain leads nowhere and it is essential to acquire the control and support of the population. The second principle states that the support of the population must be obtained through the efforts of the minority among the population that favours the counter-insurgent. The third principle states that this minority will emerge, and would be followed by the majority, only if the counter-insurgent is perceived as the ultimate victor. Therefore, it is essential for the leadership to be resolute and competent, to find supporters. The necessity for an early partial success by the counter-insurgent is obvious. The fourth principle states that seldom is the material superiority of the counter-insurgent so great that he can saturate the entire territory. The means required to destroy or expel the insurgent forces to control the population and to win its support are such that, in most cases, the counter-insurgent will be obliged to concentrate his efforts area by area. Finally, the fifth principle states that as the war lasts, the war itself becomes the central issue and the ideological advantage of the insurgent decreases considerably. The population's attitude is dictated not by the intrinsic merits of the contending causes, but by the answer to the questions: Which side is going to win? Which side threatens the most, and which offers the most protection?

Roger Trinquier, a French military officer, stated that the *sine qua non* of victory in an insurgency is the unconditional support of a population. According to Mao Zedong, it is as essential to the combatant as water to the fish. David Kilcullen, one of the world's most influential counter-insurgency warfare specialists, states that the counter-insurgency strategy should be population-centric. Therefore, it is evident that the entire counter-insurgency strategy revolves around population and measures to entice to garner its active support.

Orientation of State Policy towards Population

Kautilya argues that the wealth of the nation is in its territory and the people who follow a variety of specific occupations.[2] Consequently, the state has an important role in maintaining both the physical size of the state and the skills and interests of its population, and it is the highest duty of the king to provide security to the people while preserving the wealth of the people. To do so, state leadership is required to ensure maintenance of law and order and to uphold the fabric of the society. In other words, the state provides internal security and maintains social order for the people of the state.

Kautilya advises the leadership to pursue just and equitable economic policies that increase the revenues of the state, but does so in a manner that also increases the economic wellbeing of the populace and ensures that the needs of the people are met. "A king who impoverishes his own people or angers them by unjust exactions will also lose their loyalty."[3] Therefore, Kautilya advocates that the focus of the king's economic policies should always be the welfare of the people of the state. To emphasise the importance of the people, Kautilya states: "There cannot be a country without people and there is no kingdom without a country."[4] He then adds, "It is the people who constitute a kingdom; like a barren cow, a kingdom without people yields nothing."[5] In another passage, Kautilya says "a king who observes his duty of protecting the people justly, according to law goes to heaven, unlike one who does not protect his people, or inflicts unjust punishment."[6]

The three objectives of the *Arthasastra* are interrelated and flow one from the other; promotion of the welfare of the subjects leads to acquisition of wealth, which, in turn, makes it possible to enlarge the territory by conquest.[7] The objectives are plain. To protect the people of the state from external threats, the military is employed by the leadership to expand the state and repel invaders. To protect it from internal threats, the police power of the state maintains order, and the just magistrates of the king fairly administer the law. Economic policies are designed to increase the wealth and welfare of the population, which, in turn, increases the state treasury. In example as well as rhetoric, the king upholds the reputation and moral centre of the state. The population is ever at the focus. Kautilya states, "In the happiness of his subjects lies the king's happiness; in their welfare his welfare. He shall not consider as good only that which pleases him, but treat as beneficial to him whatever pleases his subjects."[8]

Key Elements of Counter-Insurgency Strategy

As described by Kautilya, the dominant constituents (*prakritis*) of a State include: political leadership (*svamin*), economy (*kosha*), and the military (*danda/bala*). These components form the key elements in formulation of a counter-insurgency strategy. The political leadership symbolises prestige; the economy, wealth; and the military, security. These are the pillars of a nation. They represent national interests of a state. At a micro level, for an individual, the needs are similar; every individual aspires for prestige, wealth and security. Therefore, a sound strategy should cater to the needs of the population, along with the dominant constituents of the state.

The trinity of the political leadership, the economy, and the military with direct relation to the population is a useful model that has universal application. For example, in irregular warfare, the focus of the local government, as well as the insurgents, is the population of the state, as both seek to achieve legitimacy in their eyes. The French counter-insurgency theorist David Galula states unambiguously that an insurgency is a competition between the insurgent and the government for the support of the people.[9] The insurgents approach the people of the state for sanctuary, supply and support in order to survive. If the insurgents are not able to garner the support of the population, then the chance of success is minimal. For their part, counter-insurgent operations require the judicious employment of the military to provide security and thereby acquire the support of the population to defeat the insurgency.

The financial expenditure for such operations requires the support of the population, lest the costs of security become prohibitive. Political leadership has a decisive role to play in gathering and strengthening the political will of the people to counter insurgency. The Kautilyan model would appear to hold even in modern conditions of war and insurgency. In pursuit of a counter-insurgency campaign with the stated goals of security and nation-building in countries such as Afghanistan and Iraq, the US has focused on rebuilding local economies, national military and local police forces, and legitimate political leadership with active support and involvement of the target population. Towards achieving the objective, a vital role is required by the political leadership, economy, and the military of the US, but none of this is possible without the unwavering support of the population of America. No plan for success in foreign states is possible, as Kautilya reminds us, without first attending to the needs of the population at home.

Kautilya's Seven Constituents of a State

The seven constituent parts (*prakritis*)[10] of a state, as enumerated by Kautilya, provide a framework with vital significance. They also form the elements of Comprehensive National Power. According to Kautilya, the power that a state can bring to bear in promoting its own interest vis-à-vis other states depends on how close to the ideal the constituents are. The seven constituents of a state as enumerated by Kautilya includes all elements of national power (*prakritis*): the political leadership (*svamin*), the governing body (*amatya*), the territory with people (*janapada/rashtra*), the economy (*kosha*), the infrastructure (*durga*), the military (*danda/bala*), and the allies (*mitra*).[11] A counter-insurgency strategy would include the orchestration of all instruments of the national power: political, economic, military, social, informational and diplomatic.

Intelligence—A Prerequisite for Counter-Insurgency Operations

For counter-insurgency operations, effective and timely intelligence is an inevitable requisite. Kautilya advocated creation of a secret service with spies, double agents, and specialists, to include assassins, to perform the functions: surveillance and reconnaissance over own enemy and allies; gather intelligence; provide security (internal and external); exercise vigilance over officials; ensure law and order; carry out subversion and espionage; and assassinations. The secret service was an important arm of the king to gain clarity of the internal and external situation, and exercise positive control to ensure the wellbeing of the state.

Having gathered intelligence, the counter-insurgency operations entail the detailed analysis of general political situations and recommended actions that provide a glimpse of the "genius". Kautilya advocates, forgoing short-term advantages to ensure strategic gains. Kautilya describes the intangible and unpredictable factors that affect policy choices. Kautilya lays great importance on the power of good command, analysis and judgment (genius). For specific situations, Kautilya provides four devices: relative power, deviation from the ideal, classification by the type of motivation and the influence of the intangible and unpredictable.

Kautilya's Four Instruments (*Upayas*) for Addressing Internal Threats

To accord internal security to the people, and address the internal threats in counter-insurgency warfare, Kautilya mentions the use of four ancient concepts (*upayas*) that have universal application. These concepts are:

adopting a conciliatory attitude (*sama*), placating with rewards and gifts (*dana*), sowing dissensions among enemies (*bheda*), and using force (*danda*). Conciliation (*sama*) is achieved by extolling common relationships, explaining the advantages that will accrue to each of the two parties. Placating with gifts (*dana*) is achieved by rewarding with money, granting favours, and giving employment.[12] Sowing dissensions (*bheda*) is carried out between enemies by creating mutual suspicion between them or by threatening one of them. Force (*danda*) can be used to deprive a person of his property, liberty, or life, and includes plunder, harassment, and death. These concepts can be used in isolation or combination depending on the situation. While the six measures of foreign policy are utilised by the king for statecraft, the four concepts have wider application and cross the boundaries of all.[13] For instance, Kautilya recommends that the conqueror who has secured the submission of a king should treat him with honour, unless the king harbours hostile intentions. By treating the vassal unjustly, he not only faces the prospect of retaliation but he is also likely to incur the wrath of the circle of states. The conqueror is required to respect the other kings in the vicinity of his kingdom, or they may unite and foil the conqueror's aspiration of world conquest. Therefore, it implies that the political leadership and the military should treat the surrendered insurgents justly, and this ethical behavior would go a long way in countering insurgency.

Kautilya's Six Measures of Foreign Policy for External Threats

The external threat to the state from an adversary, supporting an insurgency in a neighboring state, should be dealt in accordance to the six measures of foreign policy. Kautilya's concept of diplomacy comprises ideals of statecraft to be achieved by following a six-fold state policy to transit from a state of decline to stabilisation, and finally progress or advancement. The six-fold state policy (*sadgunyas*) comprises prudent action related to hostility (*vigraha*), peace with a treaty (*samdhi*), neutrality (*asana*), marching on an expedition (*yana*), seeking protection (*samshraya*), and dual policy of war with one state and peace with another (*dvaidhibhava*). To employ suitable policy to match the strategic environmental dynamics of political situations is the apex of diplomacy.

Four Types of War

The ultimate objective of the king is the destruction of the natural enemy, an adversary who is extending external supply, support and sanctuary to insurgency in a neighbouring state. To achieve the objective, Kautilya defines four kinds of wars to deal with such an adversary: war by counsel (*mantrayuddha*), describing the exercise of diplomacy employed by a weaker king when he considers it unwise to wage war; open war (*prakashyuddha*), specifying time and place; concealed war (*kutayuddha*), which refers to irregular warfare and psychological warfare; and clandestine war (*tusnimyuddha*), using covert methods to achieve the objective without actually waging a battle. According to Kautilya, war is the ultimate expression of state power interaction. Kautilya lists various factors that need extensive consideration before commencement of a military campaign. The factors include power (intellectual power, military might, and enthusiasm and morale), place, time, right kind of troops for mobilisation, right season and desired outcome of the campaign. Kautilya advises a king to engage in declared war, only when his military is superior, his instigations in enemy camp have been successful, all precautions against dangers have been taken and the terrain is suitable to the conqueror, otherwise, the king shall use deception in his campaign. Kautilya advocates use of psychological warfare and propaganda against enemy forces.

Conclusion

Kautilya's *Arthasastra* provides guidance to manage a state through transition from a state of decline to one of stabilisation, and from there to achieve progress or advancement. The support of the population is critical for the existence and advancement of insurgency. Therefore, the focus of statecraft should always be the safety and comfort of the people of the state—the word *artha* simply denotes the material wellbeing of the individuals. The *Arthasastra* emphasises the need for the formulation of a strategy to focus on the population. The trinity of the political leadership, the economy, and the military with direct relation to the population is a useful model that has universal application in formulation of an effective counter-insurgency strategy. The duty of the king was first towards his people, to protect them in time of natural calamities and from enemies, both internal and external. The king had a threefold obligation in this regard: protection, administration and welfare.[14] Therefore, the counter-insurgency would include political, economic, military, diplomatic and information strategies, all of which recognise and advocate the primacy of the state. This entails strengthening and judicious employment of the *prakritis*, effective use of *sadgunyas*, the *upayas* to ensure security, prosperity of the people by ensuring the efficacy of statecraft and effectively countering insurgency.

NOTES

1. R.P. Kangle, *The Kautiliya Arthasastra Part II*, Motilal Banarsidass Publishers, New Delhi, 2010, p. 512, [15.1.1-2].
2. *Ibid.*, p. 512, [15.1.1]. Explains the importance of territory for prosperity of the state to ensure welfare of the people.
3. *Ibid.*, p. 335, [7.5.27]. Describes the need for a ruler to focus the economic policies to benefit the people of the state.
4. *Ibid.*, p. 486, [13.4.5]. Explains the importance of people of the state to the ruler.
5. *Ibid.*, p. 357, [7.11.24-25]. Describes the critical role of manpower in the state machinery.
6. *Ibid.*, p. 195, [3.1.41]. Advises a king to ensure just rule of his kingdom.
7. L.N. Rangarajan, *Kautilya: The Arthashastra*, Penguin Books, New Delhi, 1992, p. 15.
8. R.P. Kangle, note 1, p. 47, [1.19.34]. Advises a ruler to accord the interests of the people, highest priority.
9. Che Guevara, *Guerilla Warfare,* University of Nebraska Press, Lincoln, 1985, p. 148.
10. R.P. Kangle, note 1, p. 314, [6.1.1].
11. *Ibid.*
12. L.N. Rangarajan, note 7, p. 113.
13. R.P. Kangle, *The Kautiliya Arthasastra Part III*, Motilal Banarsidass Publishers, New Delhi, 2010, p. 255.
14. L.N. Rangarajan, note 7, p. 118.

5

Methods and Means of Warfare: Kautilya and Contemporary Laws of Armed Conflict

U.C. Jha

Kautilya is credited with destroying the Nanda (tyrant) rule and installing Chandragupta Maurya (321-297 BCE) on the throne. Kautilya's *Arthashastra* is one of the most comprehensive treatises ever produced on state power. According to Kautilya, a king had two responsibilities to his state; internal and external, for which he needed an army. One of the external duties of the king was *raksha* or protection of state from external aggression. The other responsibility was the expansion of territory by conquest. War against enemy is defined broadly by Kautilya and not limited to only physical warfare. Kautilya regarded war as a means to an end—or an extension of policy through the application of force. However, there are number of rules in Kautilya's *Arthashastra*, resembling principles and practices to be followed under the contemporary law of armed conflict.[1] Some rules of combat found in the modern treaties, which impose restrictions on the conduct of war, the means of warfare, and their application can be traced back to Kautilya's *Arthashastra*.

Kinds of War

Kautilya advocated three kinds of warfare or fighting (*yuddha*). *Prakasayuddha* is open warfare, specifying time and place, i.e. a set-piece battle. In Kautilya's opinion, open warfare in any form was righteous. In open warfare he believed that no morals can stop the state from fighting. *Kutayuddha* is concealed warfare and refers primarily to *upajapa*, psychological warfare including instigation of treachery in the enemy camp. *Tusnimyuddha*, 'silent or clandestine war', is using covert methods to achieve the objective without actually waging a battle, implying the use of secret agents for enemy officers or killing them.[2] In waging clandestine war, the king used not only his own agents and double agents, but also allies, vassal kings, tribal chiefs and the suborned friends and supporters of the enemy.[3]

The Military Forces

The need for a loyal standing army has been stressed in the *Arthashastra*.[4] Interestingly, it was widely acknowledged that peaceful remedies should be exhausted before having recourse to the armed force. So far as the command structure was concerned, the standing army was divided into chariot, elephant, cavalry and infantry corps, further subdivided into divisions and battalions.[5] Ordnance had a parallel structure enabling it to assist all the fighting units.[6] It has been estimated that Chandragupta had an army of 600,000 infantry, 30,000 horsemen, 36,000 men with elephants and 24,000 men with chariots.[7] In recruiting, Kautilya preferred an army of trained *kshatriyas* or a large force composed of *sudras* and *vaishyas*; in his view, an enemy was likely to disarm *brahmin* troops by prostrating himself before them.[8] In addition, references to fighters on water (navy) are found[9] as well as fighting from trenches.[10]

Methods and Means of Warfare

Similar to contemporary laws of armed conflict,[11] Kautilya's laws of war were founded on the principle of humanity. The text clearly recognised the distinction between military targets, which could be attacked, and non-military persons and objects, which could not be attacked. Warfare was largely confined to combatants. The destruction of cities or towns during war was prohibited. According to Kautilya, to be in accordance with *dharma*,[12] the place and time of battle must be specified beforehand.[13] The *Arthashastra* provides a detailed description of the methods and means to be used in warfare. While the term 'means of warfare' commonly relates to the regulation of weapons, the term 'methods' covers a broader array of rules depending on the definition considered. Traditionally, with regard to weapons, 'means' encompasses weapons, weapons systems or platforms employed for the purposes of attack; whereas 'methods' designates the way or manner in which the weapons are used.[14] However, the concept of method of warfare also comprises any specific, tactical or strategic ways of conducting hostilities that are not particularly related to weapons and that are intended to overwhelm and weaken the adversary. Use of minimum forces to defeat enemy has been recommended.[15] Some of the specific provisions relating to the methods and means of warfare as described by Kautilya are as follows.

Targeted Killing

Targeted killing[16] is the intentional slaying of a specific individual or group of individuals undertaken with explicit government approval. A number of empirical studies on targeted killing suggest that targeted killing is an effective tool for stopping terrorism. Targeted killings, thus, take place in a variety of contexts and may be committed by governments and their agents in times of peace as well as armed conflict, or by organised armed groups in armed conflict. Kautilya describes how a weak king shall arrange the killing of an aggressor by one of the following means: (i) using the opportunity of a tumult, [assassin] may enter the king's chamber and kill him; (ii) using the opportunity of the king trying to escape from a tumult, selected fighters of jungle tribe may kill him from the shelter of a rampart or by ambushing him; (iii) using the confusion of an attack, agents in the guise of hunters may assassinate the enemy treacherously; (iv) [assassins] may use the appropriate method of killing the aggressor depending on the terrain and conditions such as a narrow path, a mountain, a rampart, a marsh or a water course; (v) [assassins] may drown him by breaching a dam on a river, lake or tank; (vi) if the aggressor is entrenched in a desert fort, a forest fort or a water fort, assassins may use fire and smoke to destroy him; or (vii) assassins may kill him with fire if he is in confined place, with smoke if he is in desert, with poison if he is in his own place, with crocodiles and other beasts if he is in water and with weapons if he tries to escape from a burning building.[17]

Use of Poison against Aggressor

While defending himself from a strong aggressor, Kautilya is of the view that the weak king should seek shelter, either with a more powerful king or in a fort.[18] In order to frustrate the attacks by the enemy, attempts should be made to get the chief army officers of the enemy to desert him or to get them killed.[19] If these efforts do not succeed and the enemy keeps advancing, the weak king should entrench in the fort. He is then advised to follow scorched earth policy, i.e. to burn down fuel and grass up to a distance of one *yojana* all around the fort, to spoil or drain away water and put all possible obstructions in the path of the enemy's march.[20] When a siege is laid by the strong king, various tactics should be tried to outwit him. For example, an underground tunnel may be built and officers of the enemy or the enemy himself be kidnapped, or poisoned supplies may be allowed to 'fall in the hands' of the enemy, with disastrous results for his army.[21]

Though the use of poison is prohibited under the contemporary armed conflict and its use amounts to war crime under the Rome Statute of the International Criminal Court,[22] Kautilya recommends the use of poison against aggressor: An agent in the guise of a wine seller or one serving as a chief in the aggressor's army shall be used to poison the army in its camp. The agent shall manufacture an excuse [for offering the wine] by first proclaiming a condemned man as his son and killing him with poison just before the launch of an attack by the aggressor. He shall then distribute poisoned wine liberally as a funeral libation. Or, unadulterated wine may be distributed on the first day and thoroughly poisoned wine the following day. Or, unadulterated wine may be first given to the army chiefs and then, when they are drunk, given thoroughly poisoned wine.[23] Agents in the guise of wine sellers or sellers of cooked meat, rice and cake shall attract the people in the aggressor's camp by selling high quality food cheaply, ostensibly due to mutual competition. The food and drink shall then be mixed with poison.[24] Likewise, elephants and horses in the aggressor's camp may be poisoned either by agents selling poisoned fodder or water by agents in the guise of animal attendants mixing it with grass or water.[25] Though the use of poison and kidnapping is prohibited in the contemporary armed conflict, the International Court of Justice in the Nuclear Weapon case has stated: "...the Court cannot conclude definitively whether the threat or use of nuclear weapons would be lawful or unlawful in an extreme circumstance of self-defence, in which the very survival of the state would be at stake."[26] Perhaps in Kautilya's views where a king has exhausted all the means of defence against a powerful enemy, and there is a serious threat to his life and kingdom, the use of poison and kidnapping is justified. However, Kautilya does not mention the use of poison as a weapon in *prakasayuddha* or open warfare.

Command Responsibility

According to Kautilya, the chief of defence was responsible for discipline in the armed forces (command responsibility). [He shall] be conscious [at all times] of the maintenance of discipline in the army, whether the army is camping, marching on an expedition or fighting a battle. Any official who incurs the displeasure of the people shall either be removed from his post or transferred to a dangerous region.[27] The chief commanders of various wings were responsible for the training of their troops and maintaining discipline.[28] The modern doctrine of command responsibility can be defined as the responsibility of commanders for war crimes committed by subordinate members of their armed forces or other persons subject to their control. This responsibility includes the failure to prevent or punish subordinates for unlawful actions. The Geneva Convention of 1949 CE lays down that each belligerent party bears responsibility under international law for the conduct of all members of its armed forces, and that the state is obliged to maintain discipline, law and order at all times.[29]

The Siege

When an enemy defeated in battle takes shelter in a fort, his overthrow has to be achieved by besieging and capturing it. In Kautilya's words, however, the siege was a costly exercise as it entailed losses of men, heavy expenditure and long absence from home. It was therefore necessary for the aggressor to capture the fort in the shortest possible time at a minimum cost to himself. The five means of taking a fort are: psychological warfare, enticing the enemy out, weakening him, besieging him and taking the fort by direct assault.[30] Before laying the siege, the aggressor may wage psychological war (*upajapa*) with the aim of frightening the people inside the fort and boosting the morale of his own people, subverting the enemy's high officials or depopulating the territory of the enemy.[31] If this does not succeed, the aggressor shall pry out the enemy from the protection of the fort by various clandestine methods and kill him (*yogavamana*).[32] If the enemy is intelligent and aware of these tactics, it is unlikely that he will fall for any of the tricks. Kautilya implies that those who know how to manipulate these tricks also know how to counteract them.[33] If the attempts at killing the enemy prove impractical, the conqueror shall set about weakening the enemy (*apasara*).[34] The method suggested include a trusted subordinate of the conqueror gaining the enemy's confidence and then betraying him and using allies or the enemy's enemy. The next method for the aggressor is to infiltrate his own forces into the fort, so that it can be taken from the inside. Laying siege (*paryupasana*) and taking the fort by direct assault (*avamardha*) is the last resort.[35] The right condition, the right time and the method of assault has been well defined by Kautilya.[36] On the way to the fort, the conqueror should grant safety to the people. Those who have to be removed from the place where fighting may take place should be settled elsewhere and helped in every way. Destruction of the people is a ruinous policy. For, says Kautilya in his own words, a country without people makes no sense, and there can be no kingdom without a country.[37] The following shall not be harmed when the enemy fort or camp is attacked:[38]

(a) Those who have fallen down in the fight (*patita*)
(b) Those turning their backs on the fight (*paranmukha*)
(c) Those who surrender (*abhipanna*)
(d) Those whose hair are loose [as a mark of submission] (*muktakesh*)
(e) Those who have abandoned their weapons (*muktasastra*)
(f) Those whose appearance is changed through fear (*bhayavirupa*)
(g) Those who are taking no part in the fight (*ayudhyamana*).[39]

Contemporary International Humanitarian Law (IHL) stipulates that attacking a *hors de combat* is prohibited. A person is *hors de combat* if: (i) he is in the power of an adverse party; (ii) he clearly expresses an intention to surrender; or (iii) has been rendered unconscious or incapacitated by wounds or sickness, and therefore is incapable of defending himself.[40] Additionally, Article 51 of the 1977 Additional Protocol I and Article 27 of the Fourth Geneva Convention of 1949 provide safeguards to the protected person in the occupied territory.

Treatment to Sick and Wounded in War

Protecting the sick and wounded in war was the founding principle of the Geneva Convention signed in 1864.[41] It remained the core of the IHL as it extended to other aspects of the conduct of war, now consolidated in the four Geneva Conventions of 1949, three Additional Protocols, and a series of other treaties. Regarding the treatment of the sick and wounded in war, Kautilya writes: "The following shall be stationed in the rear: physicians with surgical instruments, equipments, medicines, oils and bandages; women with cooked food and beverages to encourage men to fight."[42] Veterinary doctors were also part of the rear party to look after injured horses and animals.

Protection of Prisoners

The principles of international law on the treatment of prisoners of war (POWs), which have evolved gradually since the 18th century, are based on the principle that war captivity is neither revenge nor punishment, but solely protective custody, the only purpose of which is to prevent prisoners from further participation in the war. Kautilya advocated the humanitarian treatment of conquered soldiers and citizens. In particular, he maintained that a humanitarian policy towards defeated people was practical; pointing out that if a king massacres those whom he has defeated, he frightens all the kingdoms that surround him and terrifies even his own ministers, whereas more land and loyal subjects can be gained if the defeated are treated magnanimously. Kautilya advised that the conquering king should order the release of all prisoners and give help to the distressed, the helpless and the sick;[43] a contemporary policy contained in the third Geneva Convention of 1949 relating to the treatment of prisoners of war.[44]

Deception

The contemporary laws of war permit deceiving the enemy through stratagems and ruses of war intended to mislead him, to deter him from taking action, or to induce him to act recklessly, provided the ruses do not violate rules of international law applicable to armed conflict.[45] Under the modern IHL, deception measures which mislead enemy are permitted.[46] Ruses of war—to induce enemy to act recklessly; for example, dummy, false communication, surprise, camouflage, feigned movement of troops are allowed. Some of the measures (ruses of war) permitted under modern IHL that find mention in the *Arthashastra* are: inciting of enemy combatants to desert or mutiny or to rebel; spreading of rumour; and dissemination of misleading information affecting the morale of the adverse armed forces.

The *Arthashastra* also recommends principle of deception to provide safeguards to kings taking part in a battle. Kautilya says, troops which are brave, skilful, or of noble birth, loyal and not unhappy with the wealth and honours bestowed on them shall be placed in the centre of the forces. [Among them] the king shall take his place, bare of flags and distinguishing features and surrounded by warrior kinsmen [paternal relatives, brothers and sons]. He shall normally ride a chariot or an elephant and be guarded by cavalry; or he may ride whatever is preponderant in his army or in which he is proficient. A double shall impersonate the king at the head of the battle formation.[47]

Weapons

In the *Arthashastra*, an exhaustive list of ordnance including weapons, armour and siege machines to be used in warfare have been provided. The chief of ordnance was responsible for the safety of the equipment and was to keep an account of the weapons destroyed. Each weapon was required to bear the king's emblem.[48] The weapons which could be used in the warfare have been listed thus putting a ban on any unlisted weapons. The modern IHL also puts a limit on the means and methods of warfare: "In any armed conflict, the right of the parties to the conflict to choose methods and means of warfare is not unlimited."[49] Infantry had archers as well as soldiers equipped with swords, spears and lances for hand-to-hand combat. The list of war material found in the *Arthashastra* is as follows:

A. Fixed Machines[50]

Sarvatobhadra: A machine like a cart-wheel for throwing stones.

Jamadagnya: A machine to shoot arrows.

Bahumukha: A tower for archers (with many holes to shoot from).

Visvasaghatin: A beam, released by a mechanism, so as to fall on attackers.

Samghati: A machine with long poles to set fire to attacking mobile turrets.

Yanaka: A rotating machine to throw logs.

Parjanyaka: An engine to pump water to put out fire.

Bahu: Two pillars, released by a mechanism, to fall towards each other and block a passage or kill animals.

Urdhvabahu: A heavy pillar released by a mechanism.

Ardhabahu: A smaller version, half the length of the above.

B. Weapons with sharp points[51]

Sakti: Four *hasta* long, with a leaf shaped tip.

Prasa: Two feet long, double handed.

Kunta: A long sharp weapon for horse riders.

Hataka: Three-pointer weapon.

Bhindipala: A broad bladed weapon for horse riders.

Sula: Spear.

Tomara: Four or five *hasta* long with an arrow shaped tip.

Varahakarna: Spear with a tip like a boar's ear.

Kanaya: A throwing weapon, about two feet long, with triangular points at either end; with a grip in the middle.

Karpana: arrow-like throwing weapon.

Trasika: A two-handed weapon like the *prasa* but with a tail.

C. Mobile machines[52]

Panchlika: A wooden plank studded with nails and placed in the moat.

Devdanda: A beam, with or without nails, placed on top of the fort walls.

Sukarika: A leather bag filled with cotton or wool placed around turrets.

Musalayashti: Pike.

Hastivarka: A pike with multiple points for use against elephants.

Talavrinta: A machine to raise wind dust.

Mudgara: Hammer (thrown by machines).

Gada: Mace.

Spriktala: Mace with sharp nails.

Kuddala: Spade.

Asphatima: A catapult.

Utpatima: A machine to pull down pillars.

Udhghatima: A machine to pull down towers.

Sataghni: A mobile pillar studded with nails.

Trisula: Trident.

Chakra: Discus.

D. Bows and arrows[53]

Bows could be made of palmyra, bamboo, wood, bone or horn. The different types were: *karmuka*, *kodanda*, *druna*, and *dhanus*. Bowstrings were made of *murva*, *arka*, hemp, *gavedhu*, bamboo, bark or the sinews of animals.

E. Swords[54]

Nistrimsa (with a curved tip), *mandalagra* (straight with a rounded tip) and *asiyashti* (long and thin) are types of swords. The hilts shall be made of rhinoceros horn, buffalo horn, elephant tusk, wood or root of bamboo.

F. Cutting weapons[55]

Parasu: A scimitar, two feet long.

Kuthara: A kind of axe.

Pattasa: An axe with a trident at one or both ends.

Khanitra: Saw.

Kuddala: Axe.

Chakra: Discuss.

Kandachhedana: A big axe.

G. Stone weapons[56]

Stones could be thrown by machines, catapults or by hand. Millstones were also used as weapons.

H. Armour[57]

Lohajalika: A coat made of metal rings.

Pattajalika: Armour made of sheet metal.

Sutrakankata: Made of fabric, stuffed with cotton, wool or hair.

Note: skin, hooves and horns of dolphins, rhinoceros, bison, elephant or bull can also be used.

Types and parts of personal armour:

Sirastrana: Helmet.

Kanthatrana: Neck guard.

Kurpasa: Cuirass (breast plate and back plate).

Kanchuka: Hauberk (coat of mail up to the knees).

Varavana: Coat of woollen cloth reaching to ankles.

Patta: Sleeveless armour not made of metal.

Nagodarika: Tasset (thigh guard) or gauntlet (glove).

I. Other protective devices

Peti: Protective box or camouflage of creepers.

Charma: Protector made of leather.

Hastikarna: Board used as a cover.

Talamula: Shield shaped like the root of a palm tree.

Dhamanika: Blown up leather bags.

Kapata: Hinged wooden door.

Kitika: Cover made of leather, bamboo or cane.

Apratihata: Device to deter elephants.

Balahakanta: Same as above but with metal strips.

J. Equipment for Defence of Forts

Stored in pits along the ramparts: stones, spades, axes, arrows and implements for sharpening them, choppers, clubs, hammers, sticks, *chakras*, machines, pikes, and bamboos with sharp points, long-necked vessels for pouring hot oil as well as various kinds of forests produce necessary for defence.[58]

The use of elephant in war was recommended; accordingly elephants were trained for use during war. The training included: (i) stationary drill, standing drill; (ii) movement drill, including stopping, lying down and jumping over obstacles on command; (iii) advancing and marching in straight, transverse, zigzag or circular movements; (iv) trampling and killing horses, chariots or men; (v) fighting with other elephants; (vi) assaulting forts; and (vii) fighting with infantry, cavalry or chariots in war.

Fire as Weapon of War

Flame and incendiary weapons are the oldest weapons known to man and were used as early as 1200 BCE. However, in Kautilya's philosophy, when a fort can be captured by fighting, fire shall not be used at all. For fire is a divine calamity whose effects are unpredictable; it is a destroyer of unaccountable numbers of people as well as grains, animals, wealth, forest produce and other goods. Even when captured, a fort, whose stores are all burnt down, only gives rise to further losses.[59] The horrors of incendiary weapons impelled the negotiation of the third protocol to the 1980 UN Convention on Conventional Weapons (CCW).[60] Drafters of the protocol had serious concern with the death, disfigurement, and severe and painful injuries that incendiary weapons inflicted on civilians during the Vietnam War, Korean War and other armed conflicts. The purpose of the Protocol was to protect civilian lives by restricting the circumstances in which such weapons could be used.

Governing Occupied Territory

In the territories acquired[61] by conquest, the conqueror shall continue the practice of all customs which are in accordance with *dharma*; and shall introduce those which had not been observed before. He shall substitute his virtues for the enemy's vices and where the enemy was good, he shall be twice as good. Likewise, he shall stop the practice of any custom not in accordance with *dharma*, and shall also refrain from introducing them.[62] A conquering king should reassure the defeated people that not much have changed except their rulers. He should adopt the character, dress, language and customs of the people [of acquired territory], show same devotion to the gods of the territory [as his own gods] and participate in the people's festivals and amusements. He should honour the local deities and make grants of land and money to men distinguished in wisdom and piety. The conquering king should show his goodwill toward the defeated by instituting a righteous custom that had not previously been introduced. Kautilya commented that "one must kill a dangerous person; however, the king must leave his property untouched and shall not appropriate the land, property, sons or wives of the killed one." Any official who incurs the displeasure of the people shall either be removed from his post or transferred to a dangerous region.[63] The laws of war in ancient India with regard to occupied territory were, thus, more humane and broader than those of IHL today. The Fourth Geneva Convention of 1949 and the 1977 Additional Protocol I contemplate and contain similar obligations in the occupied territory. These are: respect to protected persons in all circumstances (their honour, their family rights, their religious convictions and practices, and their manners and customs),[64] prohibition on all acts of violence (pillage, reprisal against protected persons and property),[65] prohibition on attacks on civilian objects,[66] no change in the status of public officials or judges in the occupied territory,[67] ensuring the food and medical supplies of the population,[68] protection of cultural objects and places of worship,[69] and the protection of natural environment against widespread, long-term and severe damage.[70]

War Booty and Rewards

Kautilya also held that the fundamental rule about immoveable property was that it did not belong to the victor by right; only such things as chariots, animals and war material belonged to the conquering forces. The king should personally examine all such captured wealth and should then keep a part for himself and distribute the rest among his armed forces according to rank. The chief of defence shall make the troops happy with wealth and honours and announce the following rewards—a hundred thousand *pana*[71] for killing the enemy king, fifty-thousand for a prince or the army chief, ten thousand for a division chief, five thousand for an elephant or chariot warrior, thousand for a horse, one hundred for an infantry section leader, twenty for a soldier, as well as double normal wages and whatever booty they seize. The reward shall be made known to the leaders of groups of ten (i.e., the company, battalion and divisional commanders).[72]

Conclusion

Warfare exists in the world since the recorded history of human beings. Limitations on its conduct were close behind. The conduct of Roman war, as reported in various literatures, was unrestrained. Prisoners could be enslaved or massacred, plunder was general; and no distinction was made between combatants and noncombatants. This changed with time. In Asia, a variety of Hindu texts describe numerous rules of war. About 2,400 years ago, Kautilya gave rules of war applicable even to the contemporary armed conflict. He drew a clear distinction between civilians and belligerents; the principle found in Article 48 of Additional Protocol I, while Article 51 thereof protects civilians from military operations. Kautilya shows a deep understanding of criminal justice and war justice and advocates that defeated king shall be treated with respect and his ministers be treated humanely. Surprisingly, though a harsh realist, Kautilya advocates mercy towards the people defeated in a war, a contrast to reality of modern day conflict where principles and rules of IHL are being violated with impunity. Kautilya maintained that a humanitarian policy toward a defeated people was practical. If a king massacres those whom he has defeated, then he frightens all those kingdoms that surround him and terrifies even his own ministers.[73] Kautilya's understanding of justice, war, diplomacy and human rights makes him unique in his times. Some of his provisions were more advanced than what is visible in contemporary armed conflict. He believed that while it is as much important for the state to wage a war and conquer, it is also important to maintain law and order within the state in order to make it more powerful.

NOTES

1. The contemporary law of armed conflict (also known as the laws of war or international humanitarian law (IHL) is contained in the four Geneva Conventions of 1949, their three Additional Protocols of 1977/2005 and over 50 weapon ban or regulation treaties. The IHL is designed to regulate the treatment of the individuals—civilian or military, wounded or active—in international armed conflict. The term 'international humanitarian law' (IHL) is of relatively recent origin and does not appear in the Geneva Conventions of 1949. See: Dieter Fleck, *The Handbook of International Humanitarian Law*, Oxford University Press, Oxford, 2008, p. 11.
2. R.P. Kangle, *The Kautiliya Arthasastra Part II*, Motilal Banarsidass Publishers, Delhi, 1988, p. 342, [7.6.40-41].
3. L.N. Rangarajan, *Kautilya: The Arthashastra*, Penguin Books, New Delhi, 1992, p. 676.
4. These armed forces, however, comprised separate classes of armies including the highly trained and well-paid standing army, a less prestigious territorial army raised for particular campaigns and then demobilised, local militias and auxiliaries including tribal units and jungle tribal forces commanded by their own chiefs, allied forces and mercenaries. See: L.N. Rangarajan, note 3, p. 684.
5. Every division of the formation has its own distinguishing trumpet sound, flags and banner. These were used to signal the commands to that division, halting, advancing, turning and attacking. See: R.P. Kangle, note 2, p. 452, [10.6.46]; L.N. Rangarajan, note 3, p. 686.
6. The qualifications required for appointment to the Chief of Ordnance are not given separately. It is also not clear whether he was considered a civilian official, like the other heads of department in charge of industries, or as a defence service official. From his responsibilities it is clear that he was fully conversant with the manufacture and correct storage of all types of offensive and defensive weapons, armour and material required for secret warfare. His main responsibilities was to establish factories staffed with craftsmen expert in their fields for the manufacture of machines for attacking in battle as well as attacking enemy forts, machines for defending one's own forts, weapons, armour and accoutrements (for horses and elephants). L.N. Rangarajan, note 3, pp. 696-697.
7. Quincy Wright, *A Study of War*, (2nd ed.), University of Chicago Press, Chicago, 1965, p. 148. The numerical strength of the Mauryan armed forces has been estimated in the range of 300,000 to 600,000. See: E.J. Rapson (ed.), *The Cambridge History of India, Vol.* 1 (Reprint), S. Chand & Company, New Delhi, 1987, p. 371.
8. R.P. Kangle, note 2, p. 412, [9.2.21-24].
9. *Ibid.*, p. 180, 355, 442, [2.33.8, 7.10.34-35, 10.4.2].
10. *Ibid.*, p. 355, [7.10.36-37].
11. The contemporary law of armed conflict or international humanitarian law (IHL) can

be defined as the branch of international law limiting the use of violence in armed conflicts by: (i) sparing those who do not or no longer directly participate in hostilities; and (ii) restricting it to the amount necessary to achieve the aim of the conflict which—independently of the causes fought for—can only be to weaken the military potential of the enemy. From this definition the basic principles of IHL may be drawn, namely: the distinction between civilians and combatants, the prohibition to attack those *hors de combat*, the prohibition to inflict unnecessary suffering, the principle of necessity and the principle of proportionality. See: Marco Sassoli, Antoine A. Bouvier and Anne Quintin, *How Does Law Protect in War? Volume I*, International Committee of the Red Cross, Geneva, 2011, p. 93.

12. *Dharma* not only signifies an absolute and immutable concept of righteousness but also includes the idea of duty which every human being owes to oneself, to one's ancestors, to society as a whole and to the universal order. *Dharma* is law in its widest sense—spiritual, moral ethical and temporal. Every individual, whether the ruler or the ruled, is governed by his or her own *dharma*. To the extent that society respected *dharma*, society protected itself; to the extent society offended it, society undermined itself. [The observance of] one's own *dharma* leads to heaven and eternal bliss. L.N. Rangarajan, *Kautilya: The Arthashastra*, Penguin Books, New Delhi, 1992, p. 13, 107.
13. R.P. Kangle, note 2, p. 440, [10.3.26].
14. Marco Sassoli, Antoine A. Bouvier and Anne Quintin, *How Does Law Protect in War? Volume I*, International Committee of the Red Cross, Geneva, 2011, pp. 280-282.
15. For example, an archer letting off an arrow may or may not kill a single man, but a wise man using his intellect can kill even reaching unto the very womb. See: R.P. Kangle, note 2, p. 453, [10.6.51].
16. The term 'targeted killing' has not been defined in any of the human rights treaties. In the recent years, the tactic of targeted killing is most closely associated with Israel's campaign against the Second Palestinian Intifada. Since September 2001, the United States has also consistently conducted targeted killing operations against terrorist personnel. A number of targeted killings were reported during the Russian military operations in Chechnya in 1999. The Russian government justified the killings, claiming that they were necessitated by the fight against terrorism. In recent years, targeted killing as a tactic in the ongoing campaign against terrorism has generated considerable controversy. Some commentators view it as an indispensable tool and argue for its expanded use, while others question its legality and claim that it is immoral and ultimately ineffective. For more details see: Melzer Nils, *Targeted Killing in International Law*, Oxford University Press, Oxford, 2008.
17. R.P. Kangle, note 2, p. 469, [12.4.22-28].
18. *Ibid.*, p. 460, [12.1.1-9].
19. *Ibid.*, pp. 462-467, [12.2 and 12.3].
20. *Ibid.*, p. 471, [12.5.13-15].
21. *Ibid.*
22. Article 23(a) of the Hague Regulations of 1899/1907 prohibits the employment of

poison or poisonous weapons. The use of poison and poisonous weapons was prohibited by many ancient cultures because it was thought to be cowardly and unworthy of a warrior. The modern prohibition law is founded on the fact that as a weapon, poison is inherently indiscriminate and may cause superfluous injury or unnecessary suffering. The use of poison referred to in the document relates mainly to the poisoning of drinking water or foodstuff likely to be used by enemy forces, while poisoned weapons include poisoned arrows or spears. Article 8(2)(b)(xvii) of the Rome Statute of the International Criminal Court calls 'employing poison or poisoned weapons' a war crime.

23. R.P. Kangle, note 2, p. 467, [12.4.4-7].
24. *Ibid.*, [12.4.8].
25. L.N. Rangarajan, note 3, p. 530; See also: R.P. Kangle, note 2, p. 468, [12.4.12-13].
26. The International Court of Justice (ICJ) is the judicial branch of the UN, and the highest court in the world on general questions of international law. Article 65 of the Statute of the ICJ states that the Court may give an Advisory Opinion on any legal question at the request of whatever body may be authorised by or in accordance with the Charter of the United Nations to make such a request. Article 96 (2) of the UN Charter states that, in addition to the General Assembly or the Security Council, "Other organs of the United Nations and specialised agencies, which may at any time be so authorised by the General Assembly, may also request Advisory Opinion of the Court." In 1994, the General Assembly, sought an Advisory Opinion from the International Court of Justice (ICJ) on: "Is the threat or use of nuclear weapons in any circumstance permitted under international law?" *Legality of the Threat or Use of Nuclear Weapons*, ICJ Advisory Opinion, July 8, 1996.
27. R.P. Kangle, note 2, p. 492, [13.5.21].
28. L.N. Rangarajan, note 3, p. 692.
29. The Additional Protocol I to the Geneva Conventions, adopted in 1977, was the first international treaty to codify the doctrine of command responsibility. The provisions relating to command responsibility are contained in Articles 86 and 87 of the Protocol. *Article 86*—Failure to Act: 1. The High Contracting Parties and the Parties to the conflict shall repress grave breaches, and take measures necessary to suppress all other breaches, of the Conventions or of this Protocol which result from a failure to act when under a duty to do so. 2. The fact that a breach of the Conventions or of this Protocol was committed by a subordinate does not absolve his superiors from penal or disciplinary responsibility, as the case may be, if they knew, or had information which should have enabled them to conclude in the circumstances at the time that he was committing or was going to commit such a breach and if they did not take all feasible measures within their power to prevent or repress the breach. *Article 87*—Duty of Commanders: 1. The High Contracting Parties and the Parties to the conflict shall require military commanders, with respect to members of the armed forces under their command and other persons under their control, to prevent and, where necessary, to suppress and to report to competent authorities breaches of the Conventions and of this Protocol; 2. In order to prevent and suppress breaches, the High Contracting Parties and Parties to the conflict shall require that,

commensurate with their level of responsibility, commanders ensure that members of the armed forces under their command are aware of their obligations under the Conventions and this Protocol; 3. The High Contracting Parties and Parties to the conflict shall require any commander who is aware that subordinates or other persons under his control are going to commit or have committed a breach of the Conventions or of this Protocol, to initiate such steps as are necessary to prevent such violations of the Conventions or this Protocol, and, where appropriate, to initiate disciplinary or penal action against violators thereof.

30. R.P. Kangle, note 2, p. 491, [13.4.63].
31. Psychological warfare includes: (i) demonstrating omniscience in which the conqueror shall demonstrate his pervasive knowledge about the enemy that he is aware of their domestic affairs and secret activities [13.1.2]; (ii) demonstrating association with Gods [13.1.3-6]; (iii) propaganda by using soothsayers, readers of omen, astrologers, clandestine agents who shall advertise in the enemy's territory about the conqueror's army and wealth [13.1.7-10]; and (iv) taking action against enemy's chiefs in which the conqueror's agents in the guise of envoys pretending to be motivated by friendliness shall tell the chief principals of the enemy of the high regards the conqueror has for them, of the strength of his side and of the deterioration in the enemy's side. The principals, both civilians and military, shall be promised that they will not lose (rewards and honours when the conqueror absorbs the territory). The principals shall be looked after if they encounter calamities and be treated as father would treat his children [13.1.11-13]. See: L.N. Rangarajan, note 3, p. 729-731.
32. R.P. Kangle, note 2, pp. 477-481, [13.2].
33. *Ibid.*, p. 479, [13.2.36].
34. *Ibid.*, pp. 481-485, [13.3].
35. *Ibid.*, pp. 485-491, [13.4].
36. *Ibid.*, p. 488, [13.4.25-26].
37. While in 1863 the American Lieber Code stated that "it is lawful to starve the hostile belligerent, armed or unarmed, so that it leads to the speedier subjection of the enemy", by 1919, the Report of the Commission on Responsibility set up after the First World War listed "deliberate starvation of civilians" as a violation of the laws and customs of war subject to criminal prosecution. The prohibition of starvation as a method of warfare is codified in Article 54(1) of Additional Protocol I. This provision was generally considered new at the time of the adoption of Additional Protocol I but since then has hardened into a rule of customary international law. Under the Statute of the International Criminal Court, "intentionally using starvation of civilians as a method of warfare" is a war crime in international armed conflicts. The prohibition of starvation is set forth in numerous military manuals. Starvation of civilians as a method of warfare is an offence under the legislation of many states. This rule is also supported by official statements and other practices. This includes that of states not, or not at the time, party to 1977 Additional Protocol I. Contrary practice has been generally condemned or has been denied by the accused party. The prohibition of starvation as a method of warfare does not prohibit siege warfare as long as the purpose is to achieve a military objective and not to starve a civilian

population. See: R.P. Kangle, note 2, pp. 485-486, [13.4.2-5].

38. R.P. Kangle, note 2, p. 490, [13.4.50-53].

39. R.P. Kangle, *The Kautiliya Arthasastra Part III*, Motilal Banarsidass Publishers, Delhi, 1988, p. 260.

40. Article 41, the 1977 Additional Protocol I to the Geneva Conventions of 1949.

41. The beginning of modern IHL relates to the battle of Solferino in northern Italy between French, Italian, and Austrian forces in 1859. Henry Dunant, a businessman from Geneva, witnessed this carnage, in particular the miserable fate of the wounded left on the battlefield. He tried to alleviate the sufferings of the wounded and sick on the battlefield with the women of the surrounding villages. He invited the states "to formulate some international principle, sanctioned by a convention inviolate in character" and give a legal protection to the military wounded in the field. Dunant's proposal was successful and a small committee, the ancestor of the International Committee of the Red Cross, was founded in Geneva. In 1863, the Geneva Committee persuaded the Swiss Government to convene a diplomatic conference. The conference met in Geneva in August 1864 and adopted the "Geneva Convention for the Amelioration of the Condition of the Wounded in Armies in the Field." Thus, the modern IHL, consisting of 10 Articles, was born. The first Geneva Convention of 1949 (Article 12) provides for protection and care of wounded and sick members of the armed forces in the field. See: U.C. Jha, *International Humanitarian Law: The Laws of War*, Vij Publications, New Delhi, 2011, p. 15.

42. According to Kangle, these are not quite nurses in the modern sense of term. See: R.P. Kangle, note 39, p. 259; R.P. Kangle, note 2, p. 441, [10.3.47].

43. R.P. Kangle, note 2, pp. 491-492, [13.5.5, 10, 11].

44. The third Geneva Convention of 1949 provides certain specific rights to the prisoners of war.

45. J. Ashley Roach, *Ruses and Perfidy Deception during Armed Conflict*, 23, *U. Tol. L. Rev.*, 1991-1992, p. 395

46. Article 37, the 1977 Additional Protocol I.

47. R.P. Kangle, note 2, p. 441, [10.3.38-42].

48. *Ibid.*, p. 305, [5.3.37].

49. Article 35.1, the 1977 Additional Protocol I.

50. R.P. Kangle, note 2, p. 131, [2.18.5].

51. *Ibid.*, p. 132, [2.18.7].

52. *Ibid.*, [2.18.6].

53. *Ibid.*, [2.18.8-11].

54. *Ibid.*, p. 133, [2.18.12-13].

55. *Ibid.*, [2.18.14].

56. *Ibid.*, [2.18.15].

57. *Ibid.*, [2.18.16-17].

58. L.N. Rangarajan, note 3, p. 812; R.P. Kangle, note 2, p. 67, [2.3.33-35].

59. R.P. Kangle, note 2, p. 488, [13.4.22-24].

60. The 1980 UN Convention on Conventional Weapons, in its Protocol III on the Prohibition or Restrictions on the Use of Incendiary Weapons, states that it is

prohibited in all circumstances to make the civilian population as such, individual civilians or civilian objects the object of attack by incendiary weapons.

61. There are three ways by which a conqueror can acquire territory: by inheritance, reacquisition and conquest. The acquisition may be of two kinds—extensive, including forests and other types of land, or a single city, fort or village. See: R.P. Kangle, note 2, p. 491, [13.5.1-2]; L.N. Rangarajan, note 3, p. 741.
62. R.P. Kangle, note 2, p. 493, [13.5.24].
63. *Ibid.*, pp. 491-492, [13.5.3-21].
64. Article 27, the Fourth Geneva Convention of 1949.
65. Article 33, the Fourth Geneva Convention of 1949 and Article 51.6 of the 1977 Additional Protocol I.
66. Article 52.1 of the 1977 Additional Protocol I.
67. Article 54, the Fourth Geneva Convention of 1949.
68. Article 55, the Fourth Geneva Convention of 1949.
69. Article 53 of the 1977 Additional Protocol I.
70. Article 35.3 and 55 of the 1977 Additional Protocol I.
71. *Panas*: Silver currency units.
72. R.P. Kangle, note 2, p. 441, [10.3.45-46]
73. *Ibid.*, p. 375, [7.16.30-31].

6

Military Adages and Stratagems in Kautilya's *Arthaśāstra*

Harjeet Singh

In consideration of the works on the *Arthaśāstra* and *niti*, their value of providing an insight into the ancient Indian military system can hardly be over-estimated. It gives us the background of the system and reveals the ideas and principles on which the structure stood. Though primarily concerned with statecraft, the writers of the *Arthaśāstra* and *niti* seldom kept warfare out of their purview. They seem to have believed, like Clausewitz that "war is merely a continuation of policy by other means."[1]

It is well-known that of all the texts of this kind which have come down to us, the earliest and the most comprehensive is the *Arthaśāstra* of Kautilya. It contains the most complete statement of Mauryan ideas on governance, law and war. The problem of its age and authorship has in recent times aroused much animated discussion. There are some who believe in the hypothesis, first propounded by Shamasastry, that it is a work composed by Chanakya, the minister of Chandragupta Maurya. There are others who contend that this traditional ascription of the *Arthaśāstra* to the Mauryan minister is not justified by internal evidence and that the work could not have been composed earlier than the first or second century CE, and it cannot be considered merely the work of a *pandit*. Be that as it may, it is essentially the work of a practical administrator little interested in political theories.

Though formally a *śāstra*, it is unquestionably based on the realities of civil and military administration.[2] In regard to the age of the *Arthaśāstra*, even though it was composed before the Christian era, it largely portrays the theories and institutions of an earlier epoch. It is generally recognised that there are remarkable points of resemblance between the administrative and economic system of the Mauryas and that of the *Arthaśāstra*. Moreover, Kautilya begins his work with the statement that it is "a compendium of almost all the *Arthaśāstras* which have been composed by ancient teachers."[3] He frequently quotes opinions of previous authors and schools. It is, therefore, reasonable to assume that the ideas and customs embodied in the *Arthaśāstra* are applicable not merely to the age of its author, but also to earlier times. Thus, the military ideas and institutions of Kautilya's work could roughly pertain to the period from 300 BCE to 100 CE.

Whatever be its actual date, the *Kauṭilīya Arthaśāstra* contains a vast mass of useful information regarding the military ideas and practices of the ancient people of India. It describes the composition of the army and the relative value of its different branches. It speaks of the duties of various military officers, and defines the functions of the different arms. It contains detailed rules for stabling and training horses and elephants, for marching and camping, for fortification and siege craft. Moreover, Kautilya's maxims on tactics and strategy are, at once, wise and sound, and often remind us of the sayings of Chinese masters like Sun Tzu. Kautilya insists throughout on the necessity for constant precaution, on the avoidance of risks, on protection by means of energetic entrenching and vigilant sentries. He emphasises the need for accurate topographical information and recommends the utilisation of natural features in battles and attention to climatic and meteorological changes. He recognises the absolute necessity of a reserve in battle. Without a reserve, he categorically maintains, the king should never attempt to fight, "for it is by the reserve force that dispersed troops are collected together."[4]

It should be noted, however, that Kautilya was no warmonger by temperament. If the end could be achieved by non-military methods, even by methods of intrigue, duplicity and fraud, he would not advocate an armed conflict. He says: "When the advantages derivable from peace and war are of equal character, one should prefer peace; for disadvantages, such as the loss of power and wealth, sojourning and sin, are ever attending upon war."[5] Again, he writes: "The arrow discharged by an archer may or may not kill a single person; but skilful intrigue, devised by wise men, may kill even those who are in the womb."[6] Elsewhere, however, in an altogether different context, Kautilya says: "Whoever is inferior to another shall make peace with him; whoever is superior in power shall wage war."[7]

This brings us to the consideration of another important characteristic of Kautilya's mental make-up, viz., his predilection for fraud and duplicity, in other words, his non-moral attitude. Almost every chapter of the *Arthaśāstra* bears the impress of this Machiavellian outlook. Kautilya did not feel the slightest scruple in the employment of wine, women, poison or spies for the achievement of a goal and would not allow the intrusion of ethics into a discussion of politics and war. There is, however, one slight difference. Machiavelli stated in his *Discourses* that it is only from warfare that he would exclude ethics as irrelevant. In the *Arthaśāstra*, Kautilya tacitly warns morality from the threshold.

The *Arthaśāstra* denotes the received wisdom of India and is mooted by many to be the basis of Indian strategic culture. However, in practice, it has never been so. In its spirit of *realpolitik*, the *Arthaśāstra* deals with a system of politics or principles based on practical rather than moral or ideological considerations. In its elucidation of *machtpolitik*, the *Arthaśāstra* is vociferous in the use of power by a political state in the attainment of its objectives. It, thus, reveals an altogether surprising aspect of Indian civilisation. In practice, post-Independence India has always adopted a high moral tone in its pursuit of its foreign policy.

Kautilya lived in a period of constant warfare and realised the importance of war as an important aspect of statecraft. Both major Indian epics, the *Ramayana* and the *Mahabharata* deal with wars and treat rivalries as natural and normal. However, it is the *Arthaśāstra* which forms the foundation of intrinsic Indian strategic thought. Its basic advantage is that it is a written text as opposed to oral tradition in India. In Kautilyan terms, a nation needs to skilfully employ its strengths against an enemy weakness. The asymmetric approach to conquest was understood and approved of and it fits into contemporary pragmatic Indian culture. In this context, the Indian policy of non-alignment was directly Kautilyan (akin to *udasina* i.e. "lying outside" or the neutral king, though not indifferent to events)—a means of enhancing security by a low-risk strategy of playing one superpower off against another until India could gain sufficient strength to protect its own security interest: The ideas propounded by Kautilya are still alive in the political scene of India which is proof of his great political acumen. He developed the science of politics, as he had aspired, and we see his principles used by political scientists and defence analysts today.

Kautilya is another name for Chanakya, and in the contents of the *Arthaśāstra* we have a book written by a great scholar who played a dominant part in the establishment, growth and preservation of the Mauryan Empire. Chanakya has been called the Indian Machiavelli, and to some extent the comparison is justified. But he was a much bigger person in every way, greater in intellect and action.

Bold and scheming, proud and revengeful, never forgetting a slight, never forgetting his purpose, availing himself of every device to delude and defeat the enemy, he sat with the reins of empire in his hands and looked upon the emperor more as a loved pupil than as a master. Simple and austere in his life, uninterested in the pomp and pageantry of high position, when he had redeemed his pledge and accomplished his purpose, he wanted to retire Brahmin-like, to a life of contemplation.[8]

There was hardly anything Chanakya would have refrained from doing to achieve his purpose; he was unscrupulous enough; yet he was also wise enough to know that this very purpose might be defeated by means unsuited to the end. Long before Clausewitz, he is reported to have said that war is only a continuance of state policy by other means. But, he adds, war must always serve the larger ends of policy and not end in itself; the statesman's objective must always be the betterment of the state as a result of war, not the mere defeat and destruction of the enemy. If war involves both parties in a common ruin, that is bankruptcy of statesmanship. War must be conducted by armed forces; but much more important than the force of arms is the high strategy which saps the enemy's morale and disrupts his forces and brings about his collapse, or takes him to the verge of collapse, before armed attack. Unscrupulous and rigid as Chanakya was in the pursuit of his aim, he never forgot that it was better to win over an intelligent and high-minded enemy than to crush him. His final victory was obtained by sowing discord in the enemy's ranks, and, in the very moment of this victory, so the story goes, he induced Chandragupta to be generous to his rival chief. Chanakya is said to have handed over the insignia of his own high office to the rival minister, whose intelligence and loyalty to his old chief had impressed him greatly. So the story ends not in the bitterness of defeat and humiliation, but in reconciliation and in laying the firm and enduring foundations of a state, which had not only defeated but won over its chief enemy.[9]

The central idea of Kautilya's doctrine, as enunciated in the *Arthaśāstra*, was the prosperity of king and country and the king's quest for victory against rival neighbouring states. The king had to try to defeat his enemies one after another. Kautilya identified seven elements (*prakritis*) of state, which reinforced his ability to do so and thereby expand his own power. These were the qualities of the king, then of his ministers, his provinces, his city, his treasure, his army, and his allies. The aim of the *Arthaśāstra* was to instruct the king on how to improve the qualities of these factors and undermine those of his enemies. He showed great understanding of the weakness of human nature while enunciating his doctrine.

The Army in Mauryan Political Thought

The conception of the state as consisting of seven essential elements, of which the army was one, dates from pre-Kautilyan times, and was accepted as an axiomatic truth by all later writers. The army was, thus, accorded a recognised position in the state-organism. But it is nowhere held up as the supreme element. In contemporary thought, it usually takes rank as sixth in the order of gradation. There is a discussion in the *Arthaśāstra* as to the relative importance of the army (*danda*) and the treasury (*kosa*), and Kautilya pronounces himself definitely in favour of the latter. "The army", he says, "may go to the enemy, or murder the king himself, and bring about every kind of trouble. But finance is the chief means of observing virtuous acts and of enjoying desires."[10] Later writers, though adhering to the general principles of Kautilya, show a more positive inclination to idolise the army. Kamandaka, for instance, says that "even the foes of a king, possessing an efficient army, are turned into friends; a king with a strong army rules the earth unhampered."[11] In the *Sukraniti* the relation of the army to the state has been compared with that of the mind to the man. As without the mind the human organism cannot work, so without the army the state-organism comes to a standstill.[12] "Without the army", Sukra writes elsewhere, "there is neither kingdom, nor wealth, nor prowess. The treasury is the root of the army, and the army is the root of the treasury. It is by maintaining the army that the treasury and the kingdom prosper, and the enemy is destroyed."[13]

The *Arthaśāstra* also emphasises the role of diplomacy but shows no preference for it over war. This is simply because an important component of society of his time was the warrior group whose very existence was tied to warfare. Diplomacy, according to Kautilya, was for winning allies, delaying war if one was vulnerable, and making post-war arrangements for a new order.

The most important person in a kingdom, according to Kautilya, was the ruler. A king possessed of good character, and having the best elements of sovereignty, was the fountain of policy. He is termed the *vijigisu* (would be conqueror). Statecraft was a key factor in conquest and Kautilya framed the *vijigisu's* problem as a *mandala*—a ring of concentric circles. The *vijigisu* himself was at the centre. Next to him was likely to be an enemy plotting his destruction. Next to that enemy was that enemy's enemy, and the enemy of one's enemy is a friend. Of course, once the extant enemy was disposed of, the problem was reframed because the former ally became a probable enemy. In this ever-threatening situation, peace was preferable to war only insofar as it bought time to recover from a weak position. It was a temporary expedient, and conquest was to be resumed as soon as it was practical, whether by open warfare, pre-emptive surprise strikes, or secret sabotage. Such an aggressive foreign policy was always justified. Kautilya stated that "any king whose kingdom shares a common border with the conqueror is an antagonist."[14] This assumption is Clausewitzian strategy turned on its head—instead of all warfare being an instrument of policy; all policy is a means to prosecute war.

Shaurya (heroism) was a greatly valued virtue of a warrior in Indian thinking but to this was always added the concept of *niti* (ethical principles) in the conduct of warfare. The belief has always been that without *niti* war is merely a display of the baser instincts of mankind. For a victory based on principles (*dharmavijaya*), the king and the warriors had to observe certain codes in warfare. These codes were incorporated in the *Dharmashastras* (Books of Law) handed down from the ancient past. Warfare carried out according to the codes was also called *prakashayuddha* (open warfare). Preparations for such a war were made openly in the full knowledge of the adversary. There was no element of surprise and there were strict rules about seasons of warfare; the duration of combat was restricted to daylight hours and rigid codes about close combat between warriors were observed. There was little room for strategy or tactics; only the numbers of warriors, their skills and the quality of weaponry counted. But, at the same time, diplomacy played an important role in building alliances for war and in making decisions about whether or not to go to war.

Alongside, a strong school of *realpolitik* also existed in India. Ancient Indian thinkers produced two schools of war, diplomacy and inter-state relations; the *dharmayuddha* (ethical warfare) school; and the *kutayuddha* (devious warfare) school. These two schools were not mutually exclusive. The practitioners of each school were influenced by the principles and methods of the other and practised them. The best example is the *Mahabharata* war in which both schools of thought operated; and victory went to the practitioners of *kutayuddha*, although the war itself is described as *dharmayuddha*. In the other epic war, the *Ramayana*, although both streams of thought were at work, victory went to the *dharmayuddha* school. At the level of rhetoric, the concept of *dharmayuddha* always reigned supreme, but in practice *kutayuddha* was often the norm. The defeat of Indian kings at the hands of foreign conquerors has been attributed by many to the loss of the traditions of war-making, particularly that of *kutayuddha*.

Kutayuddha generally produces victories aimed at self-aggrandisement. Although the form was repeatedly denounced by ancient sages, it was nevertheless practised with increasing frequency, and came to be accepted as a norm. From practice, codification of devious warfare was only a short step and a comprehensive codification was undertaken by Kautilya in the *Arthaśāstra*. The term *kuta*, in the context of hunting, was used for a trap or snare. Consequently, in the context of warfare, it came to mean ensnaring or trapping the enemy. This included the use of magic spells and other occult methods. And when it came to weaponry prevalent in those days, it included the use of poisoned arrows, fire arrows and such other weapons which could bring about destruction of men and property on a large scale. Other methods included poisoning of the enemy's water sources, attack by stealth, enticing the enemy into an unfavourable position, bribery, assassinations and attacks at night.

Elsewhere, Kautilya also mentions another form of warfare—*tusnimyuddha* (silent warfare), i.e. by using secret agents for enticing enemy officers and/or killing them.[15] It, however, needs to be emphasised that the aspects enunciated in the *Arthaśāstra*, while delineating the various tactics employed in the enumerated schools are relevant to the battlefield and could be considered forms of warfare.

Organisation of the Army

Chandragupta Maurya maintained a large standing army and an efficient war office supervised it. The Army was divided into four arms i.e. *patti* or *padati* (infantry), *asva* (cavalry), *ratha* (chariots) and *hasti* (elephants). These four components headed by their respective *adyakshas* or superintendents were together called the *chaturangabala*, or the four-limbed army.

This organisation has little relevance today as modern armies have many more components and organisations. Even the command and administrative structure has metamorphosed, though the hierarchal system remains. What remains of interest is that Kautilya, in his time, also delineated the responsibilities of commanders at each level for maintaining discipline, training and equipping as well as arranging the disposition of forces in battle formations, according to the envisaged tactics.

Composition of the Army

Kautilya mentions six types of troops which could be available to a king and examines their relative merits. These are *maula* (standing army), *bhrta* (local volunteers/auxiliaries), *sreni* (organised mercenaries), *mitra* (troops of an ally), *amitra* (enemy deserters) and *atavi* (tribal levies).[16] This composition has little relevance to the prevailing practice of recruitment and military organisation today. From a historical perspective, it only gives an insight into the composition of armies in the Mauryan period.

Kautilya observed that an army composed of units recruited from diverse sources and ready to fight for plunder may be an energetic army. On the other hand, an army whose soldiers belong to the same region, caste or profession is a mighty army; it will continue to fight even if its pay is in arrears and there is shortage of food. It shows bravery even in adverse conditions and its loyalty cannot be subverted. This is a powerful and relevant argument for retaining regiments based on class composition.

Kautilya averred that the troops should, naturally, be from the warrior castes as far as possible. Lower *varna* were acceptable but the highest *varna*, the *brahmins*, were ruled out because of the Indian social system. Kautilya stated that the enemy can put *brahmin* troops out of action simply by prostrating before them and prostrating persons, by law, could not be killed.

The lower classes of society—the *vaisyas* and *sudras*—were not excluded from military service. On the contrary, they constituted the rank and file of the army, in spite of the formal law that men followed the profession of a lower caste, if they could not sustain themselves by what appertained to their own, but must never follow the profession of a higher caste.[17]

Qualitatively, troops were considered as falling under four classes, viz., *saram* (best), *anusaram* (second best), *trtiyasaram* (third in rank) and *phalgu* (weak troops). Kautilya laid down that, in drawing up a formation, the general should place the weaker troops (*phalgu*) in the forefront of each division. Then should be deployed the *trtiyasaram*, and then the best. The second best (*anusaram*) were to be placed in the rear. The reason offered for this arrangement is typically illustrative of the intensely practical nature of Kautilyan military precepts. If the weakest troops were placed in the front line, he argued, the first shock of the enemy charge would fall upon them, and not a single soldier of the better type would perish. When the enemy is, thus, engaged in an encounter with the riff-raff of the army (*phalgu-bala*), the general could manoeuvre his best troops, swoop down upon the enemy and annihilate him. Elsewhere, he advocated that the best troops should be in the vanguard, and weaker troops in the rear.

The Fort

Nowhere, perhaps, are the ancient Hindu ideas on fortification better delineated than in the *Arthaśāstra* of Kautilya, who considered the fort as one of the seven constituent elements of the state. Doubtlessly, it was not the most important, but it was more important than the treasury, the ally and the army itself. "For it is in the fort that the treasury and the army are safely kept, and it is from the fort that secret war (intrigue), control over one's partisans, the upkeep of the army, the reception of allies and the driving out of enemies are successfully practised."[18] Elsewhere, he says that the haven of the king and of his army is a strong fort.

Kautilya classified forts under four principal types, viz., *parvata* (hill fort), *audaka* (water fort), *dhanvana* (desert fort) and *vanadurga* (forest fort). The detailed descriptions of the manner in which forts were to be planned and constructed are noteworthy. However, they have been surpassed by the writings of the French General, Marshal Sebastien Vauban (1633-1707 CE) who was the leading military engineer of his own age and arguably the best known, whose impact on fortification and siege craft was enormous. His *Treatise on Sieges and the Attack of Fortresses* (1704 CE) is a military masterpiece whose importance hinges also on the fact that he was a practical exponent of the art of constructing and besieging fortresses.

Administration

Kautilya recognised that an army is dependent on a strong finance for its upkeep. He averred that finance is necessary to undertake any state endeavour and is the chief means for both *dharma* (righteous duty) and *kama* (enjoyment). Kautilya attached great importance to the necessity for regular and liberal scales of pay for the army. Accordingly, an army must feel that it enjoyed an honourable place in society; otherwise, its morale would suffer and it could not remain efficient.

It was the duty of *nayakas* to ensure that the men were paid regularly and that correct scales of rations for the men and fodder for the animals were being drawn and correctly utilised. The actual disbursement of dues was carried out under the supervision of *senapatis*. Men and animals were issued 32 days rations every month in order to make up minor shortfalls and give *senapatis* a little reserve to be used at their discretion for extra issues when and where needed. Kautilya laid down various scales of pay for officials in the state according to their rank and grade.

Conduct of Warfare

Types of Wars

Kautilya envisaged five kinds of war to wage, which he advised the ruler to optimally utilise his resources (*prakritis*) in accordance with the *sadgunya* and the *upayas*. The five kinds of war were:

(a) *Prakashyuddha*, i.e. Open War:[19] This was advocated to be fought in accordance with the norms of *dharmayuddha* or righteous war.

(b) *Kutayuddha*, i.e. Concealed War:[20] This was recommended in circumstances where the *vijigisu* is not superior to the enemy and the terrain and season were not favourable. Various forms of *kutayuddha* have been mentioned in the *Arthaśāstra*. Here the conduct of the war involved the use of devious methods as opposed to *dharmayuddha*. It implied that there were no restrictions on its conduct and principles gave way to expediency. However, the conduct of the war still devolved on military principles.

(c) *Tusnimyuddha*, i.e. Silent War:[21] In this kind of war, the use of secret agents was recommended. This war was in sharp contrast to the previous two types of wars. The use of devious methods was its hallmark.

Two other types of war also find mention in Kautilya's *Arthaśāstra*. These are:

(d) *Mantrayuddha*, i.e. Diplomatic War:[22] This was a recommended methodology for a weaker ruler. It does not refer to actions on the battlefield but off it, and was to be conducted furtively. It involved the use of conciliation (*sama*) and gifts (*dana*) amongst diplomatic efforts as a prelude or precursor to actual fighting. Nevertheless, the use of subterfuge was not ruled out.

(e) *Gudhayuddha*, i.e. Secret War:[23] This was a variation of *kutayuddha*. It involved employing irregulars to wage war against a nation while outwardly the state is enjoying regular diplomatic ties. It could be akin to cold war norms or proxy war where covert violence, assassination and other means were employed to weaken the enemy.

Strategic Means

Kautilya enunciated four forms of strategic means (*upayas*) against enemies, in order of usage:

- Conciliation (*sama*)
- Gifts (*dana*)
- Dissension (*bhed*)
- Coercion (*danda*)

Before starting on a campaign, the king was to satisfy himself that he was superior in all essential factors to the enemy against whom he proposed to march. These included energy, bravery and personal drive of the king himself, material resources consisting of treasury and army, and good counsel and diplomacy, besides the knowledge about the terrain and topography of the enemy territory and the season. At the same time, the king was advised to take great precautions to ensure that, in his absence, no insurrection occurred. The overwhelming factor for the consideration of the king for any invasion was that what benefit or gain would accrue from the expedition and the possible losses.

Planning a Campaign

Warfare implies the conduct of systematic military operations. It is distinguished above all by one identifying characteristic—organisation. Kautilya's most striking doctrine is his discussion of planning a campaign. He describes the factors to be considered before the king decides that it is in the state's interest to commence the campaign. These include:

(a) Relative strengths of power, place and time
(b) Seasons for marching on a campaign
(c) Employment of troops
(d) Revolts and possibility of a rebellion in the rear
(e) Calculation of losses, expenses
(f) Likely dangers of treachery
(g) Assessment of dangers
(h) Overcoming of dangers

There were also detailed instructions for the marching and protection of the Army during a campaign.

Combat

Although Kautilya expended much energy in describing the various formations and battle arrays for the conduct of combat, it does not seem that they had any decisive influence on the conduct of battles. An impression rests that, after the first plunge into the fighting, there was little order in the conduct of combat. The *Arthaśāstra,* in Book X, nevertheless, does lay down dictums for the conduct of combat, e.g.:

- He who is possessed of a strong army, who has succeeded in his intrigues, and who has applied remedies against dangers, may undertake an open fight, if he has secured a position favourable to himself; otherwise he should engage in a treacherous fight.[24]
- He should strike the enemy when the latter's army is under troubles. He who has secured a favourable position may strike the enemy entangled in an unfavourable position. He who possesses control over the elements of his own state may, through the aid of the enemy's traitors, enemies and inimical wild tribes, make a false impression of his own defeat on the mind of the enemy who is entrenched in a favourable position, and having thus dragged the enemy into an unfavourable position, he may strike the latter.[25]
- When an enemy's army is compact, he should break it by use of his elephants. When the enemy has moved from its favourable position, following the false impression of the invader's defeat, the invader may turn back and strike the enemy's army, broken or unbroken. Having struck the front of the enemy's army, he may strike it again by means of his elephants and horses when it has shown its back and is retreating. When an attack on one side is unfavourable, he should strike it on the other.[26]
- The beginning of an attack is the time for treacherous fights. As to an open or fair fight, a virtuous king should call his army together, and, specifying the place and time of battle, address them. His minister and priest should encourage the army.[27]
- The army should be arrayed on a favourable ground, facing other

than the south, with its back turned to the sun, and capable to rush as it stands. If the array is made on an unfavourable ground, horses should charge. If the army is arrayed on an unfavourable position or is confined or is made to withdraw (by the enemy) it will be subjugated. The nature of the ground in the front, sides and the rear should be examined. On even ground, the staff-like or circular array should be made; and on an uneven ground, arrays of compact movement or of detached bodies should be made.[28]

- Having broken the army (of the enemy), the invader should seek for peace. If the armies are of equal strength, he should make peace when requested for it. If the enemy's army is inferior, he should attempt to destroy it, but not that which has secured a favourable position and is reckless of life.[29]
- That army which is vast and is composed of various kinds of men and is so enthusiastic as to rise even without provision and wages for plunder when told or untold; that which is capable of applying its own remedies against unfavourable rains; that which can be disbanded and which is invincible for enemies; and that, of which all the men are of the same country, same caste, and same training, is (to be considered as) a compact body of vast power.[30]
- The conqueror should know the comparative strength and weakness of himself and of his enemy; and having ascertained the power, place, the time of marching and of recruiting the army, the consequences, the loss of men and money, and profits and danger, he should march with his full force; otherwise, he should keep quiet.[31]
- Of the two things, slight annoyance in the rear and considerable profit in the front, slight annoyance in the rear is more serious; for traitors, enemies, and wild tribes augment on all sides the slight annoyance which one may have in the rear. The members of one's own state may be provoked about the acquisition of considerable profit in the front.[32]
- On acquisition of gains, economic, political, etc.—through military success: When profits (from two sources) are equal, (a wise king) should consider the place and time, the strength and means (required to acquire it), affection and disaffection (caused by it), intrigue and absence of intrigue (involving it), its nearness and distance, its

present and future effects, its constant worth or worthlessness, and its plenitude and usefulness; and he should accept only that profit which is possessed of most of the above good characteristics.[33]

- On the four forms of strategic means or *upayas* (*sama, dana, bheda* and *danda*): Of these means, that which comes first in the order of enumeration is, as stated in connection with "invaders", easier than the latter. Conciliation is of single quality; gift is two-fold, since conciliation precedes it; dissension is three-fold, since conciliation and gift precede it; and conciliatory coercion is four-fold, since conciliation, gift, and dissension precede it.[34]
- Destruction of the people is a ruinous policy. For, a country without a people makes no sense, and there can be no kingdom without a country.[35]

Battle Tactics

It may appear that, while much ingenuity was expended on the formation of battle-arrays, it did not have a decisive influence on the conduct of battles. A general impression is that, after the first engagement, there was little order maintained on the battlefield and that it was a combat of duels and push. However, in the *Arthaśāstra,* a clear enunciation of some fundamental principles of tactics is mentioned, which shows that commanders of armies followed some definite plan in conducting a campaign. For instance, it is laid down that when an army is drawn up in battle-order, the general must not move it *en masse* against the enemy but should rather assail the latter with one or two divisions; and when the enemy is thrown into confusion, should follow up the first onset with the remaining divisions. A second principle enunciated is that a commander must begin a battle by striking that portion of the hostile army which is occupied by weak and treacherous troops. Third, it is emphasised that he should make a rear-attack on the enemy, when a frontal attack is considered disadvantageous. Similarly, when an attack on one wing or flank is deemed unwise, the other wing or flank may be assailed. Having struck the front of the hostile army, the commander should follow it up by an attack from the rear. He may also strike at the enemy's rear, and then, when it has wheeled round, he must attack it from the front. Finally, a commander must not press hard a weak but desperate foe, secure in a strong position; for "when a broken army, reckless of life, resumes its attack, its fury becomes irresistible."[36]

Highlighting the importance of time and place, Kautilya mentions that: "In daytime the crow kills the owl. At night the owl kills the crow." Thus, the time of fight is important. Similarly, "A dog on land, drags a crocodile; and a crocodile in water, drags a dog," to emphasise that the place of fight is important.[37]

Espionage

Surveillance of the enemy is as old as humanity. Kautilya's *Arthaśāstra* attaches great significance to intelligence not only about the enemy, but also about citizen attitudes towards power. Spies had an important role in both the civil and military affairs of ancient India. The Kautilya's *Arthaśāstra* provides us with a graphic account of the activities of spies. They were primarily divided into two classes, viz., local agents (*samsthah*) and wandering or travelling supervisors (*samcarah*). To the former category belonged spies under the guise of a 'fraudulent disciple' (*kapatika-chhatra*), recluse (*udasthita*), householder (*grhapatika*), merchant (*vaidehaka*) and ascetic practising austerities (*tapasa*); while under the latter group came spies called 'class-mate' (*satri*), 'fire-brand' (*tiksna*), poisoner (*rasada*) , and 'mendicant woman' (*bhiksuki*).

The mention of monks, ascetics and mendicant women as spies provides an eloquent commentary on Kautilya's religious attitude. Though a *brahman*, and certainly a believer in the established order of society, he feels no hesitation in advocating an unscrupulous exploitation of the religious susceptibilities of the people. There were to be five institutes of espionage, controlling the entire intelligence department, and checking and verifying the reports coming from different sources. Cipher writing was to be used by the spies, and carrier pigeons were to carry secret intelligence.[38]

The secret service (*gudhapurusha*) had three principal strategic objectives. First, it kept the ruler informed of developments within and without the empire. Second, it conducted covert operations aimed at undermining both internal and external enemies. Third, it was mandated with the maintenance of the internal discipline and loyalty of the bureaucracy and military. A major operational principle not to be violated, except in cases of extreme emergency, was that intelligence reports from three different sources were needed for the state to authorise action.

There were numerous duties which the spies had to perform. They were to watch the conduct of government officials of all ranks, from the highest to the lowest. They were to keep the king informed about the trend of public feeling in the kingdom. They were to detect sedition and crime, and assist in the administration of justice. And last, but not the least, they had to collect accurate information regarding the state of affairs in neighbouring kingdoms, discover and foil the ruses of the other side and neutralise its successes.[39]

Broadly speaking, in relation to foreign states espionage took three forms, viz., political, diplomatic and military. Various forms of political espionage of this kind have been elaborated by Kautilya in Book I, Chapter 14, Book VII and Book XII. Diplomatic espionage was carried on by ambassadors and diplomatic agents in foreign courts.

Military espionage consisted in the employment of secret agents to procure accurate information regarding the military resources of the hostile state, plans and movements of the hostile army, and safeguarding one's own camp and army from the poisonous contamination of enemy spies; Kautilya speaks of "spies who are residing as traders in the enemy's forts, and those that are living as cultivators in the enemy's villages, as well as those who are living as cow-herds or ascetics in the district borders of the enemy's country."[40] Further, Kautilya advocates the employment of spies along with the marching army, in the camp, and also in the fighting line. They were also to harass the enemy, create divisions in their ranks, and demoralise the hostile king. In the work of espionage, all methods were admissible—spying, lying, bribing, poisoning, woman's wiles and the assassin's knife.

Contemporary Military Relevance

Modern warfare is differentiated from its earlier forms by the expansion of technology. War is a constituent element of the history of mankind. Control of armed forces rests with the state, which is able to limit the use of the armed forces when it controls violence. The margin of superiority is generally assumed to determine the degree to which violence can be limited. It is also generally accepted that the degree to which a margin of superiority is predominant, the less likelihood of it being challenged through war. Also, if there is a challenge, the greater the margin of superiority the more quickly can the challenge, in theory, be suppressed and less sustained the violence would be. The rationale for having strong armed forces is, thus, axiomatic. Kautilya understood this and enunciated many military strategies in the *Arthaśāstra*. He does not make much distinction between military strategy and statecraft. He believed that warfare is an extension and an integral part of statecraft.

In an increasingly complex world, the missions of the armed forces are more diverse and complex than ever before. The challenges today constitute diverse problems such as proxy war, insurgency, terrorism and unresolved border issues. However, the march of time has not changed the fundamentals of warfare. In times of peace and tension, the armed forces are a powerful instrument of the nation's foreign policy. In times of crisis and conflict, they are the foremost expression of the nation's will and intent. Thus, the expectations of a nation from its military are diverse and wide-ranging. Modern warfare encompasses military, political, economic and the diplomatic aspects. Warfare continues to be based on principles and precepts to be followed and applied. These verities are eternal.

According to Kautilya, the most important factor in planning and decision-making for conducting a military campaign is power. Force in present day warfare encompasses tangible (personnel, weapons, mobility, fire power and logistics) and intangible elements (leadership, morale, discipline, training, doctrine and motivation, etc.). The easiest aspects of military affairs to quantify are weapons and their effects. Weapons have well-known and easily measurable physical characteristics; they obey the standard laws of physics. It is the variables of combat which bring the intangible elements into play. The human element is given the highest importance by Kautilya. The intangible human elements are difficult to quantify and tend to tilt the balance if not correctly assessed. Hence, to compare two opponents as emphasised in the *Arthaśāstra*, their power in all aspects needs to be compared.

The *Arthaśāstra* is not only concerned about making conquests. It also discusses the strategies and tactics for the prevention of conquest by others.

Thus, a large portion of the book is devoted to statecraft and administration of the state. But, whether in conquering others or in preventing conquest, the *Arthaśāstra* takes a conflictual relationship between states as the norm. Therefore, management of these occupies an important place in Kautilya's thinking.

Despite the great similarities between the ideas of Sun Tzu and Kautilya, there remains one major difference which has to do with the different social systems of India and China. Sun Tzu's idea was: "subjugating the enemy's army without fighting is the true pinnacle of excellence."[41] Such a doctrine would have been inconceivable for Kautilya because that would have devalued the entire hereditary warrior *varna*. For them, it was a disgrace to die anywhere except on the battlefield. A world without war was, even theoretically, inconceivable to Kautilya.

Kautilya argued that national interest should override moral principles inasmuch the moral order depends upon the continued existence of the state. Yet, Kautilya never advocated the conquest of lands outside of South Asia. This line of thought is still visible in modern Indian foreign policy. India has never taken the initiative to invade a foreign country, and it has never shown interest in areas beyond South Asia.

Kautilya warns against calamities which adversely affect the functioning of the army which include not giving due honours, insufficient salaries and emoluments, low morale, etc. He makes an incisive observation that an unhonoured army, an unpaid army, or an exhausted army will fight if honoured, paid and allowed to relax but a dishonoured army with resentment in its heart will not do so.

An analysis of most insurgencies in the world shows that Kautilya was accurate in his belief that the greatest cause of insurgencies was societal discontent and advocates that the state should attach great importance to the wellbeing of the people—"if they become impoverished, they become greedy and rebellious." He also averred that "an internal rebellion is more dangerous than an external threat because it is like nurturing a viper in one's bosom."[42] Rebellions (insurgencies) were classified based on the affected region and who were their sponsors. The similarities in the methods used today and those espoused by Kautilya are striking.

Conclusion

The *Arthaśāstra* is a key text on Indian strategic culture, from the military point of view, based entirely on the role of power. For Kautilya, power was the means and not the end. "Strength is power, and happiness is the end. [...] Hence a king shall always endeavour to augment his own power and elevate his happiness." For the augmentation of power the general rule is that "whoever is inferior to another shall make peace with him; whoever is superior in power shall wage war."[43] Thus, power was the basis for the acquisition of more power.

In today's world, the challenges of global security are no different from those that vexed the Mauryan Empire in 300 BCE. A cogent and dispassionate analysis of the *Arthaśāstra* reveals stark similarities between the problems faced by Kautilya's ideal state and the modern scourge of terrorism and insurgencies. Present day warfare adheres to ancient patterns. The truism that "those who forget the lessons of history are condemned to repeat it" applies in military affairs. If a society seeks to live in peace, it should be prepared for war; a unilateral desire for peace cannot ensure peace.

Kautilya regarded the period before the actual fighting began as critical to the outcome. It was vital that the ruler and his advisors be able and willing to undertake a dispassionate and rational appreciation of the total assets of their state in relation to the enemy (or enemies), modified by the contributions of allies. Thus, geography, timing, seasonal variations, mobilisation schedules, preparing for internal rebellions and discontent, estimating material losses in relation to strategic gains, and the risks involved to the stability of the dynasty, all had to be carefully weighed. There was no point in attacking a more powerful state without first consulting one's allies. Similarly, committing troops to a limited engagement without factoring the possibility of escalation and the likely losses was to be avoided. While the military was trained and drilled into believing in itself, for the ruler and his advisers, optimism was a dangerous and potentially catastrophic luxury. Indeed, for Kautilya, the power of perspicacious advice was greater than military strength; and by combining superior intelligence and comprehension of politics, the conqueror could prevail against militarily more powerful adversaries.

The *Arthaśāstra* is testimony to the constant and unchanging nature of war. Studies of military history show that certain features of conflict and warfare constantly recur; that relationships between type of action and success often remain the same; that certain circumstances and moments have, time and time again, proved decisive. The past being a prologue underscores the relevance and significance of studies of military history such as propagated by the *Arthaśāstra*. It also underscores an ancient verity with regard to the relationship of a state and its society—that anything cannot be crushed by a blow from without until it is ready to perish from decay within.

NOTES

1. Carl von Clausewitz, *On War* (trans. Michael Howard and Peter Paret), Oxford University Press, Oxford, 2007, p. 28.
2. This double character of the *Arthaśāstra* is asserted in the text itself: R.P. Kangle, *The Kauṭilīya Arthaśāstra Part II* (2nd ed.), Bombay University Press, Mumbai, 1969, pp. 92-96, [2.10].
   Sarva-śāstra-nukramya prayogam-uplabhya ca
   Kautilyena narendrarthe sasanasya vidih krtah [2.10.63].
3. R.P. Kangle, note 2, pp. 5-10, [1.2.1-1.4.16].
4. *Ibid.*, pp. 445-449, [10.5].
5. *Ibid.*, pp. 342-345, [7.7.1-31].
6. *Ibid.*, p. 453, [10.6.51].
7. *Ibid.*, pp. 321-324, [7.1].
8. Jawaharlal Nehru, *The Discovery of India,* Penguin Books, New Delhi, 2010, pp. 125-126.
9. *Ibid.*
10. R.P. Kangle, note 2, pp. 388-389, [8.1.47-52].
11. Kamandaka, *Nitisastra,* Book XIII, Chapter 37.
12. Sukracharya, *Nitisastra,* Chapter I, Section II, pp. 122-124.
13. *Ibid.*, Chapter IV, Section II, pp. 28-29.
14. R.P. Kangle, note 2, pp. 327-330, [7.3].
15. *Ibid.*, p. 342, [7.6.40-41].
16. *Ibid.*, p. 409, [9.2.1].
17. In the light of recent researches related to early Indian society (cf. S. C. Bhattacharya, *Some Aspects of Indian Society from c.2nd century BC to 4th century AD*; B.D. Chattopadhyaya, *One Blind Man's View of an Elephant: Understanding Early Indian Social History*), it is difficult to describe these two social groups entirely as 'the lower classes of society'. There were hierarchies in both the groups. Probably among the *vaisyas* and *sudras*, there were many who possessed great strength, could be better: *bahula-saram va vaisya-sudra-balamiti.* See: R.P. Kangle, note 2, p. 412, [9.2.24].
18. R.P. Kangle, *Ibid.*, pp. 314-317, [6.1].

19. *Ibid.*, p. 339, [7.6.17].
20. *Ibid.*
21. *Ibid.*, p. 342, [7.6.40-41].
22. *Ibid.*, p. 461, [12.1.17].
23. *Ibid.*
24. *Ibid.*, pp. 417-419, [9.4].
25. *Ibid.*, pp. 427-432, [9.7.].
26. *Ibid.*, pp. 438-442, [10.3]. See: Sections 150 and 151.
27. *Ibid.*
28. *Ibid.*, pp. 442-444, [10.4]. See: Section 153.
29. *Ibid.*, pp. 428-429, [9.7.23-41].
30. *Ibid.*, pp. 409-410, [9.2.3-5].
31. *Ibid.*, pp. 406-409, [9.1]. See; Section 135.
32. *Ibid.*, pp. 413-414, [9.3.1-10].
33. *Ibid.*, p. 419, [9.4.24].
34. *Ibid.*, p. 425, [9.6.56-61].
35. *Ibid.*, p. 417, [9.4.2-5].
36. R. Shamasastry, *Kautilya's Arthashastra*, Low Price Publications, Delhi, 2012, p. 397, [10.3.57].
37. *Ibid.*, pp. 407-408, [9.1.26-33].
38. *Ibid.*, pp. 21-27. [1.11, 1.12].
39. *Ibid.*, pp. 36-39, [1.16].
40. *Ibid.*, pp. 467-469, [12.4].
41. Ralph D. Sawyer, *The Complete Art of War* (trans. Sun Tzu's Art of War), Westview Press, Colorado, 1996, p. 50.
42. R.P. Kangle, note 2, pp. 427-432, [9.7].
43. *Ibid.*, p. 319, [6.2.30-32].

7

One Year of *Arthasastra*: Response, Pedagogy and Research

P.K. Gautam

The first set of initiatives to revisit Kautilya's *Arthasastra* was done in the period 2012 and 2013. My monograph based on my fellow's seminar of 2012 was published in 2013.[1] In parallel, the first national level seminar was organised in October 2012 followed by another workshop in April 2013.[2] The proceedings of the October 2012 seminar were soon made available on YouTube and had a wide circulation and a good number of 'hits'. This chapter surveys the state of knowledge one year after the initial events. This chapter will present the experience of interaction and study of the text on three broad themes of response, pedagogy and research. I also use my monograph specially in the research part under 'Some Findings'.

Response

This exercise in revisiting traditional indigenous knowledge beginning with Kautilya has been a truly creative event since the October 2012 inaugural and icebreaking workshop followed by a vocabulary workshop in April 2013. As is mentioned, the book of these two events in one volume is now available titled *Indigenous Historical Knowledge: Kautilya and His*

Vocabulary—Volume I. The joint work of a dozen or more scholars may be a standard for further research. Over and above these edited book(s), a number of publications on various themes and concepts on Kautilya's *Arthasastra* have been produced or are in the process of being published by Indian scholars, both from the IDSA and outside. Most of the work is not on recycling what is already known or re-publishing old work but conceptual reinterpretation of contemporary issues. The field is innovative, level and wide open with many opportunities for multidisciplinary work, both by the seasoned and the young.

Networking with International Scholars

Apart from Indian scholars—in order to have the level of interaction elevated to the international—we had networked with top international scholars of the *Arthasastra* including scholars fluent in Sanskrit and ancient Indian texts, and Indologists such as Thomas Trautmann (Professor Emeritus of History and Anthropology, University of Michigan, USA); Sheldon Pollock, Arvind Raghunathan (Professor of Sanskrit and South Asian Studies Columbia University in the City of New York, General Editor, Murty Classical Library of India, Harvard University Press); Dr. Michael Liebig, Goethe University, University of Frankfurt, Germany; Rashed-Uz-Zaman, Department of International Relations, Dhaka University, Bangladesh; Jean-Claude Galey, (Directeur d'études Anthropologie sociale chez École des hautes études en sciences socials. EHESS Grande Ecole, School for Advanced Studies in Social Sciences, France)[3]; Patrick Olivelle, Professor of Sanskrit and Indian Religions and the Jacob and Frances Sanger Mossiker Chair in the Humanities at the University of Texas at Austin, USA; Mark McClish, Assistant Professor of Religion, Birmingham-Southern College, Birmingham, Alabama, USA and Balbir Singh Sihag, Professor Emeritus of Economics, University of Massachusetts, USA.

Patrick Olivelle has recently further refined Kautilya's *Arthasastra*, fifty years after R.P. Kangle's seminal translation and study of the *Arthasastra*. Patrick Olivelle's message to the IDSA was: "I am encouraged by the renewed interest in this seminal work after languishing for many years after the publication of Kangle's edition and translation in the 1960s."

Sheldon Pollock wrote to IDSA: "Your project sounds like an excellent one, and I wish you and your colleagues all success." Professor Thomas Trautmann was unable to attend the international seminar on Kautilya in India as he was working on a project on kings, elephants, and mahouts—to write the history of this interesting inter-relationship from India all the way to Persia and Greece.[4]

Efforts by Scholars of Sanskrit

Sheldon Pollock had written an op-ed in *The Hindu* in which he called this vanishing scholarship and associated skills with Indian classical languages as cultural ecocide.[5] Calcutta University has conducted research programmes on the subject. The late Asoke Chatterjee, Shastri Professor of Sanskrit, Calcutta University in his *Studies on Kautilya—Vocabulary* (1990)[6] mentions that he had guided a number of MPhils and PhDs on Kautilya. Moreover, in the same university since 2007, under the University Grants Commission (UGC), a Special Assistance Programme (SAP) work is in progress on "Principles of Governance, Management and Administration in Kautilya's *Arthasastra.*" A dictionary as an output of that endeavour is forthcoming.[7] It will be worthwhile to network with such departments.

Dearth of Interpretative Work

There is a dearth of work on application and reinterpretation by contemporary political scientists, analysts and scholars. Barring a few self-taught individuals, this effort is missing. While most scholars in the education system have been 'trained' in humanities, social and life sciences, and technical subjects, none, barring few scholars of Sanskrit or ancient history, have been trained in the *Arthasastra*.

Although Indologists equate the *Arthasastra* to a library of Indian knowledge, not much interpretative work exists in political science and International Relations (IR) to understand the ideas of strategy, military theory, and diplomacy. Demand for this type of knowledge exists with the 'consumers' such as policy-makers, planners, researchers and the academic community. This demand can be met.

Pedagogy

This section will narrate the discourse of Kautilya including reactions as understood during interactions and presentations based on issues of defence, foreign policy, war and internal security.

High Expectations with Low Results

At times, it is expected that the *Arthasastra* will provide quick answers to crisis media situations in IR that keep appearing and popping up on a multitude of media channels, subject-to-subject and day-to-day. Kautilya's *Arthasastra* is an ancient text which needs to be studied, reinterpreted and re-examined critically (version 2.0 in popular jargon) and then concepts extracted for contemporary use. If Kautilya could come forward in a time machine he would have probably lectured that "three powers or *saktis* operate in state." He would have repeated that "*prabhavasakti* (power of army and treasury) is more important than *utsahasakti* (power of personal energy) and that *mantrasakti* (power of counsel and diplomacy) is more important than both." These are not ideas, concepts and theories. They are the practical implementation and governance issues. While there may be a lot of literature and sane advice (*mantrasakti)* and the best leadership may be elected (*utsahasakti*), all will come to naught in absence of *prabhavasakti*—(economic growth, defence and security, etc.). To strengthen the comprehensive national power, ensure to get rid of the *vyasanas* as in Book VIII—Concerning Topic of Calamities of the Constituent Elements.

Assuming Knowledge of Mahabharata is Enough

Due to absence of teaching secular aspects of religion and not studying all knowledge emanating from religious literature, we are missing out on many aspects of philosophy.[8] In an interaction on Kautilya's *Arthasastra* with senior officers from a para-military organisation, it appeared that there was an opinion that all that is needed to be known is available in the *Mahabharata*, whereas this is not the case, especially on issues of statecraft.[9]

Example of Use of Indigenous Vocabulary

At the smaller scale, it may be now necessary to apply vocabulary and concepts from Kautilya's *Arthasastra*. Along with other indices, military power of a nation is a very important constituent of the nation's Comprehensive National Power. During a talk held in Delhi, a few years ago, Ashley Tellis spoke on the importance of military power. He said, "States cannot become great powers, unless at some level, they demonstrate mastery over the creation, deployment and the use of military force in the service of national objectives."[10] It may be possible to express the same idea of comprehensive power using Kautilya's *Arthasastra*. Kautilya, as we noted, says that "three powers or *saktis* operate in state—*prabhavasakti* (power of army and treasury), *utsahasakti* (power of personal energy) and *mantrasakti* (power of counsel and diplomacy)." Surely now as an exercise in method and pedagogy it may be possible to paraphrase and replace the thinking of the likes of Ashley Tellis with Kautilya with the *saktis* so described to convey a similar message.

Research

Research Questions

Conceptually, some research questions identified are listed for this deliberation at Appendix A. Not all could be addressed due to reasons of shortage of time, and non-availability of scholars. The lack of basic awareness in absence of working knowledge of the text as it relates to IR and social science was another factor. The list is not comprehensive and many more questions may be added. It is being reproduced here to share the types of question that came to mind initially. As work on this progresses, many more questions and puzzles can be framed for further research.

Some Findings

1. *Harappan Link and Influence that Radiated from India*

Tales from the *Panchatantra* have influenced the *Arthasastra* and vice-versa. Recent literature traces few of the roots to the pre-Vedic Harappan age. The dialogues and interaction of the fox and the crow provide simple lessons on national interests and outmaneuvering, so natural to diplomacy. The painted pot from Lothal of the Indus Civilisation depicts the scene of a bird perched on a tree holding a fish, and a fox-like animal below. Ancient historian and archaeologist B.B. Lal argues that the scene is very reminiscent of the story of the 'clever fox' narrated in the *Panchatantra*, wherein the fox praised the crow on the tree-top for its sweet voice and, thus, made it open its mouth and drop the morsel which the fox ran away with.[11]

To the East

The *Arthasastra* and its variations such as the *Panchatantra* also helped in the spread of Indian culture and concepts both to the East and West. The concepts such as *mandala* explained in the *Arthasastra* and other related ideas had travelled to Southeast Asia. Between 200 BCE and 500 CE in Southeast Asia, people first settled in large nucleated communities and organised themselves into small warring polities. *Mandala*, to be sure, means alliance based spheres of influence. In Thailand, the concept of *chakravartin* indicates that *chakra* or wheel (a symbol of sovereignty) of state chariot rolls everywhere without obstruction. It is believed that Mauryas developed the concept of *chakravartin*, which was incorporated into Buddhist tradition. Early Indonesian societies which adopted either Buddhism or Hinduism shared fundamental assumption about ideal political structure. Inscriptions refer to kingdom as *mandalas*, a Sanskrit word with a wide range of meaning. Its simplest connotation is a circle. One inscription engraved at Palembang by the ruler of Srivijaye in the 680s, refers to the outlying polities called *mandala* that he claimed to have brought under his control.

Niti of the old Indian rulers as embodied in such treatises became in course of time a system coveted and adopted by foreign potentates. It was exported chiefly in the form of *Beast Fables* which after the decline of Buddhism became a manual par excellence of statecraft for lands outside as well as within the bounds of the peninsula. As Buddhism waned, the collection became *nitisastra*, instead of *jatakas*. Books such as *Panchatantra* and the *Hitopadesa* were compiled not as *sutras* or as literature of entertainment, but as instructions for the princes in leading a virtuous and idealistic life.

To the West: Arabic and Persian Sources

Key ideas and concepts on issues of diplomacy and strategy from *Arthasastra* were also made into simple instructions for potential kings and for good moral conduct into a book called *The Panchatantra* (also spelled as *Pancatantra)*, whose author Vishnu Sharma acknowledges the debt owed to Kautilya's *Arthasastra. The Panchatantra*, puts into fables for early education of princes and would be statesmen, adopts the term *Nyaya-Sastra* to denote the literature.[12] Such treatises were adopted by foreign potentates and were exported chiefly in the form of books such as *Panchatantra/Beast Fables*. One example on foreign policy in the *Panchatantra* Book III is on policy deliberations on war between the crows and owls. Here the six measures of foreign policy or options of *sadgunya* (peace, war, change of base, entrenchment, alliance and duplicity) are demonstrated.[13] One such Persian collection in Pahlavi, known as *Qalila wa Dimna*, passed to Arabia and thence, along the highway of a conquering Islam, to North Africa, Spain and Provence.[14] In Spain, it was translated into Hebrew and then into Spanish in 13th century. The Hebrew version was also translated into Latin at the end of that century and published in Germany in 1480 CE, as the source for the 1483 CE *Buch der Weisheit* (*Book of Wisdom*). It was then translated into Italian in 1552 CE and English in 1570 CE.[15] The intellectual currents from India is best captured by the medieval Arab poet from Baghdad called al-Sabhadi, who said that there were "three things on which Indian nation prided itself: its method of reckoning, the game of chess, and the book tilted *Kalila wa Dimna*."[16]

There is also a vital link of this literature to poetry. The twelfth century Persian poet, Farid at-Tair, who is known for his work *Manteq at-Tair,* in his *The Conference of the Birds,* uses devices of birds for an explanation of human behaviour. The sources used are Sanai's *Divan* and also *Kalila and Dimna*. This extraordinary popular work, also called *The Fables of Bidpai*, originated in India and was translated into many languages.[17]

Sadly, the original *Panchatantra*, composed in Sanskrit, is reported to have been lost.[18] But there is some hope. Chandra Rajan, translator with an introduction to *The Panchatantara* (1993), mentions that the original 870H (1491 CE) archives of *Kalila wa Dimnah* (the Arabic version of *Panchatantara* done in Iran in 870 CE) is in National Museum New Delhi. It was inscribed and illustrated in India.[19]

2. *The Puzzle of Chanakyaniti*

What is the difference between *Chanakyaniti* literature (also called *Chanakya-sutra*) and that of the Kautilya's *Arthasastra* as fixed by Shamasastry and later improved upon by authors such as R.P. Kangle and Patrick Olivelle?

While working on *Arthasastra*, I also noticed that some authors pick up (without any consideration of scholarship or authenticity) quotes from a text claiming to be 'Kautilya's *Chanakyaniti*' (a very condensed version differing from author to author) from the internet and to sound profound ascribe it to Kautilya. Interestingly, such type of works are the most-read as they are cheap and even available at railway station book stalls. To an average reader, these types of products appear as if they existed in the original aphorism/*sutras* (*sutras* are half sentences or aphorisms or concise statement of a principle, a maxim or adage) of the *Arthasastra.* Some sutras do tally with the *Arthasastra* but not all. None of the serious scholars of the *Arthasastra,* I believe, could provide a satisfactory answer to their origin and authenticity. I have failed to locate the archival material of these *sutras* or the final authentic repository of them.

So, what is *Chanakyaniti* as we know today which in 21st century appears to be a free of all remixing and twisting of *sutra* of Kautilya? One hope is that the Tibetan *Tanjur* collection may be having what is called *Canakaraja Niti.*[20] Probably the work has not been re-translated back to its original language as yet. Nevertheless, an answer to the relationship was found by way of serendipity or a 'happy accident' or 'pleasant surprise'. This is covered next in the section on Arabic and Persian sources.

Arabic and Persian Sources

According to historian S.A.A. Rizvi, "A very comprehensive Arabic *Mirror for Princes* entitled *Siraju'l-muluk* was compiled in 1122 CE by Abu Bakr Muhammad bin al-Walid al Turtushi (1059-1127 CE), who was born in Spain and had visited Iran and Iraq. Here he met the Seljuq vizier Nizamu'l-Mulk Tusi (1018-92 CE) and was greatly impressed by Tusi's scholarship and political acumen. Even the earlier *Mirror for Princes* had drawn upon stories in *Kalila wa Dimna*, as translated from Pahlavi (old Persian) by Ibnu 'l-Muqaffa' (died 756 CE). Turtushi's work also shows a definite debt to the same source, *Kalila wa Dimna*. He refers also to *Muntakhabu'l-jawahir* (*Selected Gems*), composed by the Indian, Shanaq (Chanakya), as a guide for the monarch. This text, the *Kitab Shanaq fi al-tadbir*, was in fact the celebrated *Chanakyaniti*, a collection of political aphorisms in Sanskrit, not to be confused with the *Arthasastra* ascribed to Kautilya or Chanakya."[21]

Turtushi and Chanakyan Thought

Turtushi compared the benefits accruing from sultans to such natural phenomenon as rain, wind, the seasons, day and night, and described tyrants as worse than ravaging lions. However, he preferred even the latter to anarchy, maintaining that the good which emerged from the king outweighed any evil perpetuated by him. In a maxim attributed to Chanakya, Turtushi encouraged rulers to act like the sun, moon, earth, rain, wind, fire, water, and death. From some Hindu sources, Turtushi presented the widespread analogy of the big fish eating smaller fish and claimed that this unstable situation was averted only by a monarchy.[22]

Yet, where is the manuscript and text of the *Chanakyaniti* preserved and who is the final academic authority on its authenticity may remain a puzzle.[23]

3. Influence of Kautilya on Akbar

Abul-Fazl'Allami (1551-1602 CE) was inspired by a need to rationalise the broadly based policies of peace and concord with all religious communities initiated by his patron, Akbar the Great. Besides Arabic and Persian works of kingship and government, Abul-Fazl' Allami had access to the Persian translations of the great Hindu epics, the *Mahabharata* and the *Ramayana*, to the Arabic translation of the *Chanakyaniti* and to the Sanskrit works of ancient Indian *rajaniti* (polity).[24] The *kotwals* during Akbar's reign had many functions including taking census of towns and villages, gathering daily intelligence, movement of visitors, deterring imposters, control of bazaar activities, supervising state minting, road safety, recovering stolen property, etc. Interestingly, their duties included eradicating unemployment and investigating the source of income of those who spent money extravagantly, prevent unwilling widows from being incinerated on their dead husband's funeral pyre. S.A.A. Rizvi argues with a clear logic that "many of these provisions seem to echo the practices of the ancient Hindu kingdoms, as reflected in the text as the *Arthasastra* attributed to Kautilya. It is possible that Akbar was influenced to some extent by Hindu advisers."[25] Surely, this must have been the evidence in Panikkar's mind when he alluded that the Hindu kings, to the last followed organisation of Mauryan Empire in its three essential aspects—the revenue system, the bureaucracy and the police. This organisation was taken over by Muslim rulers; and in the British period, his doctrines were still in force.[26]

4. Mixing Up Mahabharata and Kautiliya Arthasastra to Caricature a Stereotypical Indian Strategic Culture

The *Mahabharata* which includes the *Gita* (book 6 about the battle and felling of Bhisma[27]) is a very powerful spiritual and philosophical text. It is deeply ingrained not only in the national imagination and psyche but also across the world. There exist varieties of individual or personal, regional and cultural interpretations.[28]

While the *Mahabharata* is sublime and spiritual and deals comprehensively with *dharma* and one's self realisation as given in the *Gita*, it was worrying to see a totally twisted interpretation of Indian strategic culture based on a very shallow and superficial reading of the traditional texts. George J. Gilboy and Eric Heginbotham in *Chinese and Indian Strategic Behaviour: Growing Power and Alarm* (2012) have based their work on a limited interpretation of the *Mahabharata* and *Gita* and that of Kautilya's *Arthasastra*. It is argued by them rightly that Kautilya's *Arthasastra* is the most important contribution to strategy. But they make unsubstantiated assumptions, which indicate that they have done only a selective reading and interpretation when they compare it with the *Mahabharata*. They argue, without engaging with any text, that there exists a more violent, less compromising tradition (here the authors mean *Mahabharata*). The authors continue to say that whereas Kautilya emphasises both political flexibility and military mobility, the *Mahabharata* emphasises annihilation of the enemy through systematic attrition.[29] This manufactured ethos of annihilation of a purported Indian strategic culture is a very serious matter. The authors have not given any textual interpretation or any reference as evidence to the conclusion they arrive at. It must be corrected and set right. Such incorrect and simplistic caricaturing gives a totally wrong picture of Indian traditions, culture and strategic culture and also that of the *Mahabharata* and the *Gita*. How the authors construct the entire structure without even referring to tomes of literature on *Mahabharata* may remain a mystery. Such 'parsimonious' interpretation of the *Mahabharata* by Western scholars is an incorrect and caricatured interpretation. I would suggest the Western readers or those not familiar with it to read one of the first translations of the epic into English language by Romesh C. Dutt.[30] Dutt explains that the *Mahabharata* is like the Iliad of India and it is an encyclopaedia of life and knowledge of Ancient India.[31] Another good work is *The Mahabharata* by Chakravarthi V. Narasimhan.[32]

Notwithstanding this major flaw in the work of George J. Gilboy and Eric Heginbotham, one needs to appreciate an appealing and relevant issue: that is the authors argue that Kautilya's *mandalas* apply to relationship of power, influence and interest, not only to geographic proximity.[33] Here, basing it on Rangarajan's study, they are indeed correct. This makes it possible, as explained by Rangarajan, to apply *mandala* theory with *sadgunya* and *upayas* in today's maritime matters, relationship with distant countries and impact of globalisation and information and communication technologies (ICT). A theoretical framework of "Death of Distance" by neo-geographer such as Robert Kaplan is already developed.[34] The challenge is application of the *Arthasastra* in maritime matters which would require much more effort and focus using indigenous text. It is said that "scholars, military officers, and strategists in China and India may actually be imbibing and paying heed to modern Western literature on international relations and strategy—in some cases perhaps more so than their own respective texts."[35]

5. *A Response to a Criticism of Kautilya*

To those familiar with scholars of the *Arthasastra* in India, a few with military background are dismissive of Kautilya. This has been alluded to in my monograph. For example, Major Bhakri goes to the extent of calling *matsya nyaya* and doctrine of *mandala* theory as twin evils.[36] Lt. Gen. Satish Talwar (Retd.) argues that "Kautilya's teaching led to an inflexible stance in our thinking."[37] The most detailed and scholarly work has been accomplished by Major General Gurcharn Singh Sandhu (Retd.) author of

A Military History of Ancient India (2000) and *A Military History of Medieval India* (2003).[38] "Kautilya's *Arthasastra*", Sandhu says, "is such a brilliant, comprehensive and logical work on art of governance that later writers have only endorsed its teachings and written commentaries on select aspects of it." The conservative teachers (*acharyas*) of military science, Sandhu argues, "tried to turn the art of war into a predictable game of cause and effect. They discouraged innovation and the exercise of initiative in battle. Kautilya is a prime culprit."

Apparently, Sandhu first classifies Kautilya's work as brilliant, and then blames the successive generation of teachers in being overawed by his work leading to rigidity. Surely, this is not Kautilya's fault. Many teachers improved upon the *Arthasastra*, especially Kamandaka (also known as Kamandaki) of the Gupta period, the author of *Nitisara* as explained in a 2010 article by the historian Upinder Singh of Delhi University.[39] Exclusion of Kamandaka's *Nitisara* is a serious flaw in Sandhu's work. The very exercise of reinterpretation of indigenous knowledge is to discern enduring principles both deontological and consequentialist. All classics have many central messages and the present generation has to revisit them. Let me end with an example of the flawed logic of Sandhu. Take the case of air power which developed early on 20th century. Does it mean that only theorist who wrote after the advent of air power need to be read and those who wrote before the invention of aeroplane be rejected? I, thus, reject the opinion of Sandhu as it relates to the arguments he puts forth on Kautilya's *Arthasastra*.

Conclusion

In one year, it is clear that there has been some progress. The study needs to be made wider and related to vocabulary with a critical interpretation for current national and international system. This appears to be within reach if efforts such as these are undertaken regularly and progressively.

NOTES

1. P.K. Gautam, *One Hundred Years of Kautilya's Arthasastra*, IDSA Monograph No.20, July 2013.
2. Since published as Pradeep Kumar Gautam, Saurabh Mishra and Arvind Gupta (eds.),

Indigenous Historical Knowledge: Kautilya and His Vocabulary—Volume I, Pentagon Press, New Delhi, 2015.

3. His student from France Mr. Jean Langlois-Berthelot interned to research on Kautilya at the IDSA for six months in 2013. See Jean's chapter "Kautilya's Teachings on How to "Create" Loyal Soldiers in One's Side but Sedition in the Enemy's Army", in Volume I of this series, and review of Patrick Olivelle's book *King, Governance, and Law in Ancient India*, Oxford University Press, New York, 2013, in *Strategic Analysis*, 37(6), November-December 2013, pp. 758-760.
4. I thank Professor Patrick Olivelle in providing this news.
5. Sheldon Pollock, "The Real Classical Languages Debate", *The Hindu*, November 27, 2008.
6. Asoke Chatterjeee Sastri, *Studies on Kautilya—Vocabulary*, Parimal Publications, Delhi, 1990. I thank the library staff at Asiatic Society, Kolkata for providing me this book and other information that helped me locate the department of the late author and in meeting some of his former pupils.
7. I thank Dr. Didhiti Biswas from Sanskrit Department, Presidency College, Kolkata in giving me this information during my visit to the university in April 2013.
8. This type of education of approaches to study of religions is called "Phenomenology." Phenomenological epoch is an approach to the study of religions to become and remain entirely neutral about what is studied. See: Sushil Mittal and Gene Thursby, "Introduction", in Sushil Mittal and Gene Thursby (eds.), *Religion in South Asia: An Introduction*, Routledge, New York, 2006, pp. 10-11.
9. (a) This aspect has been covered by me in my monograph and also in P.K. Gautam, *Shruti and Smriti: Some Issues in the Re-emergence of Indian Traditional Knowledge*, IDSA Issue Brief, February 12, 2013, available at http://idsa.in/issuebrief/ShrutiandSmriti_PKGautam_120213

   (b) Appendix B gives a similar example in the field of Science and Technology.
10. Talk by Air Chief Marshal N.A.K. Browne, PVSM, AVSM, VM, AD Chairman Chiefs of Staff Committee and the Chief of Air Staff, tilted "Air Power and the IAF's Strategic Transformation", IDSA, September 23, 2013, available at http://idsa.in/keyspeeches/AirPowerandtheIndianAirForce
11. B.B. Lal, "The Indus Civilization," in A.L. Basham (ed.), *Cultural History of India*, Oxford University Press, Oxford, 1998, pp. 11-19.
12. K.P. Jayaswal, *Hindu Polity: Constitutional History of India in Hindu Times, Parts I and II*, The Bangalore Printing and Publishing Company Limited, Bangalore, 1967, p. 6.
13. *Panchatantra* (34th ed.), translated from Sanskrit by Arthur W. Ryder, Jaico Publications, New Delhi, 2011, p. 234.
14. Shashi Tharoor, *Pax Indica: India and the World of the 21st Century*, Allen Lane/Penguin, New Delhi, 2012, p. 161.
15. Daya Kishan Thussu, *Communicating India's Soft Power: Buddha to Bollywood*, Palgrave Macmillan, New York, 2013, p. 49.
16. As quoted in Amartya Sen, "Indian Traditions and the Western Imagination", *Daedalus: Journal of the American Academy of Arts & Sciences*, 126(2), Spring 1997, pp. 1-26.

17. Afkhan Darbandi and Dick Davis, "Introduction", in Farid ud-din Attar, *The Conference of Birds*, translated with an introduction by Afkhan Darbandi and Dick Davis, Penguin, London, 1984, p. 9,16.
18. Kaushik Roy, *Hinduism and the Ethics of Warfare in South Asia*, Cambridge University Press, New Delhi, 2013, pp. 148-149.
19. Chandra Rajan, "Foreword", in Visnu Sarma, *The Panchatantra*, translated from Sanskrit, Penguin Books, New Delhi, 1993, p. xiv.
20. *D.D. Kosambi: Combined Methods in Indology and Other Writings*, Oxford University Press, New Delhi, 2002, p. 679, (compiled, edited and introduced by Brajadulal Chattopadhyaya). Evidence is also available in Suniti Kumar Pathak, *The Indian Nitisastras in Tibet*, Motilal Banarsidass, Delhi, 1974.
21. S.A.A. Rizvi, *The Wonder that was India Volume II: A Survey of the Indian History and Culture of the Indian Sub-continent from the Coming of Muslims to the British Conquest 1200-1700*, Picador, London, 2005, p. 156. (First published in 1987).
22. *Ibid.*, p.157. The state of anarchy or "big fish eating smaller fish" has been analysed in P.K. Gautam, "Overcoming the Ways of *Matsya Nyaya*", *Strategic Analysis*, 37(5), September-October 2013, pp. 521-525.
23. See: Research question (i) in Appendix B.
24. S.A.A. Rizvi, note 21, pp. 160-161.
25. *Ibid.*, pp. 160-161, 190-191.
26. K.M. Panikkar, *A Survey of Indian History* (3rd ed.), Asia Publishing House, Bombay, 1947, Reprint 1960, p. 29.
27. Bhishma is called *Kuruvriddha* (aged Kuru).
28. Gita is the essence of the ponderous four *Vedas*, 108 *Upanishads*, and six systems of Hindu philosophy (mere 700 concise verses). See: "Introduction", *God Talks with Arjuna: The Bhagavad Gita—Royal Science of God-Realization: The Immortal Dialogue between Soul and Spirit,* A New translation and commentary by Parmahansa Yogananda, Volume I, California, Self Realization Fellowship, 1995, p. xviii. This work is in two volumes.
29. George J. Gilboy and Eric Heginbotham, *Chinese and Indian Strategic Behaviour: Growing Power and Alarm*, Cambridge University Press, New Delhi, 2012, p. 29.
30. Romesh C. Dutt, *The Ramayana & The Mahabharata*, J.M. Dent & Sons Ltd, London, 1910, last reprint 1969.
31. *Ibid.*, Epilogue to the *Mahabharata* by the translator, pp. 323-333.
32. Chakravarthi V. Narasimsimhan, *The Mahābhārata*, Motilal Banarsidass Publishers, Delhi, 1999.
33. George J. Gilboy and Eric Heginbotham, note 29, p. 31. L.N. Rangarajan argues in his introduction to the chapter on Kautilyan Foreign Policy that "In trying to understand Kautilya's analysis, we have to keep in mind the fact that it is essentially theoretical." See: L.N. Rangarajan, *Kautilya: The Arthasastra*, Penguin Books, New Delhi, 1992, p. 506.
34. Robert Kaplan, *The Revenge of Geography: What the Map Tells Us About Coming Conflicts and the Battle Against Fate,* Randon House, New York, 2012, p. 116.
35. George J. Gilboy and Eric Heginbotham, note 29, p. 37. Authors surely have in their minds Alfred Thayer Mahan (naval power), Sir Halford Mackinder (land power),

Nicholas Spykman (rim land/coast), etc.

36. S.K. Bhakri, *Indian Warfare: An Appraisal of Strategy and Tactics of War in Early Medieval Period*, Munshiram Manoharlal Publishers, New Delhi, 1981, p. 207.
37. Satish Talwar, "The Enemy Within", *The Journal of the United Service Institution of India*, CXL(578), October-December 2009, pp. 508-512.
38. Gurcharn Singh Sandhu, *A Military History of Ancient India*, Vision Books, New Delhi, 2000; and *A Military History of Medieval India*, Vision Books, New Delhi, 2003.
39. Upinder Singh, "Politics, Violence and War in Kamandaka's Nitisara", *The Indian Economic and Social History Review*, 47(1), 2010, pp. 29-62.

APPENDIX A

RESEARCH QUESTIONS

a. What are the nuances that may be missing in the Western discourse on International Relations as existing in the *Arthasastra*?

b. Is there an Indian sub-continental/Indic discourse of International Relations? What are its key features?

c. What is the status of study about the diplomatic history of India's various kingdoms and empires over the last 2,500 years basing it on the *Arthasastra* and its variations?

d. What are *Arthasastra's* recommendations on maintaining territorial unity and integrity? What is the concept of a nation or a state?

e. Kamandaka's *Nitisara* is based on the nectar of the *Arthasastra*. What is the continuity and what are the changes as it relates to aspects of defence, diplomacy and security?

f. What is the state of research on the *Arthasastra* of Kautilya. The last works done were by Sanskrit scholar R.P. Kangle in 1960s and the English translation by Dr. N.P. Unni of the work done by Ganapati Sastri in Sanskrit. Has any new archival material come to notice? What is the state and location of archives?

g. Who are the Indologists, Scholars of South Asian Studies, linguists and historians of ancient India with knowledge of Sanskrit working on Kautilya outside India (South Asia, US, UK, Germany, France, Italy, Russian Federation, Japan, China or any other country)? If so, which departments are undertaking the work? Are young scholars pursuing the study? Is there a national and international database?

h. It is said that the political and social conditions no longer exist for the traditional way of continuation of the knowledge of the *Arthasastra*. What is the way to preserve this rich text with its nuanced interpretations?

i. In popular 'street level' discourse often *Chanakyaniti* or *Chanakyasutra* is better known than the *Arthasastra*. It is also used as a rhetorical device. Book shops in Delhi, for example, have this title with a number of pamphlet-like publications—the authors of which do not appear to be known for any worthwhile work on the *Arthasastra* at the national or international level. Most of the *sutras* of such work when compared with those of the text of the *Arthasastra* are not at all from the *Arthasastra*, rather they are shockingly twisted. This is problematic and no satisfactory answer has been found. What is the status and understanding of *Chanakyaniti*? Where is the authentic archival work now available? Who wrote or compiled it during which period? Where is the last and the latest authentic work available?

j. How does the *mandala* theory take into account (with globalisation propelled by information and communication technologies) the geographical idea of neighbourhood projected to distant neighbours?

k. What is the understanding of strategic culture when seen from the perspective of South Asian subcontinent? Is there any evidence of the *Arthasastra* in political behaviour? What is the role of historical texts such as the *Arthasastra* in the formulation of Indian strategic traditions?

l. How does the US and China fit in the idea of either *udasina* or *madhyamika*?

m. How can we explain some of the following current events and developments using ideas and logic from the *Arthasastra*:

    i. Sino-Indian relations and the border tensions in Ladakh of April 2013.

    ii. The String of Pearls theory of China and its counter.

    iii. The Asian pivot/rebalancing concept of the US. Does it anyway resemble the concept of wheel and spoke of Kautilya?

n. Is there any role of the *Arthasastra* for understanding Indian foreign policy in West Asia, Southeast Asia and East Asia (Look East Policy), Central Asia and other regions of the world? Can the *Arthasastra* suggest any better ways to deal with the different regions of the world?

o. The literature on the subject area 'Kautilya and Intelligence', focuses on intelligence collection, intelligence organisation, intelligence operations (covert operations), but not on intelligence analysis. What are the matters of intelligence analysis or synthesis that can be discerned from the *Arthashastra* in the academic discipline of intelligence studies?

p. What are the issues of Ecology and the Management of Natural Resources in Kautilya's *Arthasastra*?

q. What is the knowledge of the *Arthasastra* as it relates to Art of War for contemporary times?

r. How does the *Arthasastra* relate to asymmetrical warfare?

s. How does the *Arthasastra* relate to counter-insurgency?

t. What is the contribution of the *Arthasastra* to the composition of an army?

u. How does the *Arthasastra* contribute to military strategy and operational art today?

v. How can one relate the concepts in the *Arthasastra* to the maritime and naval domain?

w. What is the relevance of concepts in the *Arthasastra* to space and cyber security?

x. What can the *Arthasastra* contribute to peace research, conflict prevention and resolution?

APPENDIX B

ALL KNOWLEDGE OF SCIENCE AND TECHNOLOGY IS IN THE VEDAS?

In the field of science and technology, the tendency to assume that all that is to be known is already known in Indian traditions must be critically examined. One reason as to why did India lag behind in science and technology in recent centuries has been attributed to the belief that all knowledge is in the Vedas (See: B.M. Udgaonkar, "Why Did Early Indian Science not Fulfil its Promise?", in Lalit K. Kothari and Ramesh K. Kothari (eds.), *Vision and Values—Science, Defence, Education, Ethics: Essays in Honour of Dr. D.S. Kothari on His Birth Centenary*, Paragon International Publishers, New Delhi, 2007, pp. 59-96). Some reasons for not having a scientific renaissance in India despite such a strong scientific tradition put forth are: caste ridden social organisation, political upheavals, absence of medieval universities, emphasis on preceptor-disciple relationship, or importance given to spiritual pursuits over the life-sustaining values as well as a general mind-set towards being in harmony with nature. All of these would have led India to choose or prefer the already determined pathways of traditional scientific thinking (See: B.V. Subbarayappa, "Pioneers of Science and Nationalism in India", in B.V. Subbarayappa (ed.), *Science in India: Past and Present*, Popular Prakashan Pvt. Ltd./Nehru Centre, Mumbai, 2007, pp. 285-286). Joseph Needham known for "Needham's Paradox" on a similar problem in China had placed the blame in China on "bureaucratic feudalism". For the case of India, in a foreword, his guesses were: wars and colonialism, social and economic factors. However, P.C. Ray (first historian of Indian Sciences) argued in his hypothesis that the main cause of the decline of the scientific spirit in India was the entrenchment of caste society, with its disastrous degradation of the social status of the technicians, craftsmen and other manual workers. This, P.C. Ray thought, took place when Brahmins reasserted their supremacy on the decline and expulsion of Buddhism. See: Joseph Needham, 'Foreword', in Debiprasad Chattopadhyaya, *History of Science and Technology in Ancient India: The Beginning*, Firma KLM Pvt. Ltd., Calcutta, 1986, p. 9.

How can this question be tackled? Social scientists in India rightly argue that till historians do not engage with the history of science in India, the Needham's paradox may be the defining interpretation based on a Western understanding of Indian traditions.

Index